JAMES W. CORTADA is the author of several books on the history of Spanish-American diplomatic relations.

VERA C. WINKLER has written numerous articles for both newspapers and journals and is currently working for the United States Government.

A SPECTRUM BOOK

THE WAY TO WIN IN GRADUATE SCHOOL

James W. Cortada/Vera C. Winkler

PRENTICE-HALL INC., Englewood Cliffs, New Jersey 07632

Library of Congress Cataloging in Publication Data

Cortada, James W
    The way to win in graduate school.

    (A Spectrum Book)
    Bibliography: p.
    Includes index.
    1. Universities and colleges—Graduate work—
Handbooks, manuals, etc. I. Winkler, Vera C.,
joint author. II. Title.
LB2371.C596   378.1 553   78–10659
ISBN 0–13–946202–3
ISBN 0–13–946194–9 pbk.

Editorial/production supervision and interior design by Norma Karlin
    and Jeannette Jacobs
Cover design by Anne Winslow
Manufacturing buyers: David Hetherington and Cathie Lenard

A SPECTRUM BOOK

10 9 8 7 6 5 4 3 2 1

Printed in the United States of America

Prentice-Hall International, Inc., *London*
Prentice-Hall of Australia Pty. Limited, *Sydney*
Prentice-Hall of Canada, Ltd., *Toronto*
Prentice-Hall of India Private Limited, *New Delhi*
Prentice-Hall of Japan, Inc., *Tokyo*
Prentice-Hall of Southeast Asia Pte. Ltd., *Singapore*
Whitehall Books Limited, *Wellington, New Zealand*

To
Dora and Ed

Contents

viii
_____
Contents

Preface

Today over 250 universities grant Ph.D. degrees in nearly one hundred fields, and an ever larger number of schools offer an M.A. in more numerous areas. Approximately 700,000 students attend graduate schools in the United States despite recent financial cuts by universities and a decline in federal aid to higher education. Regardless of reports to the contrary, the number of students declined only slightly throughout the 1970s even in the face of university cutbacks. The figures for 1977 and 1978 reflect a similar pattern. Many students seek and will continue to attend, graduate schools in large numbers regardless of the job market or shrinking academic budgets.

This book, designed to help students who either want to go to American graduate schools or who are already in advanced degree programs, was written from the student's point of view, since the authors were graduate students when they wrote it. A student quickly learns that his peers are often the best source of information regarding professors, finances, courses, and programs. This is a guidebook of such time-tested student wisdom. The book offers part of this knowledge to students before they enter graduate school and to those who have just commenced their studies in order to help them avoid the common mistakes of others—mistakes which often waste time and incur needless expenses. The many guides to American graduate schools are written mostly by professors who tend to talk down to their pupils. Others, issued by educational councils, often fail to answer questions raised by students; instead, they discuss what professors think graduates worry about. Since students, as a rule, cannot afford to invest many dollars in such manuals, which are usually expensive, it is our purpose to offer an inexpensive guide at a price well within the means of all students.

Preface

Many generalizations have been made that may not apply to a given graduate program. This cannot be helped because we are attempting to reach a large number of students. However, we have tried to test our comments by having students in various fields read and correct our mistakes. Medical and law students have not been specifically dealt with here simply because their graduate studies differ fundamentally from the traditional M.A. and Ph.D. programs. But some chapters do deal with problems that are relevant to medical and law students and have been reviewed by students working in medicine and the law.

We would like to express our thanks to the many people who have helped us, either by teaching us along our way in school or by commenting on the manuscript. Among these are students at Florida State University, at the universities of Florida, Wisconsin, California (U.C.L.A.), Minnesota, Pennsylvania, and Massachusetts, and at Princeton University and Harvard University. Our special gratitude goes to Michael Hunter and his staff at Prentice-Hall for moving our book smoothly and expeditiously through to publication. Any weaknesses and inaccuracies are our own, for which we acknowledge responsibility.

J.W.C.
V.C.W.

1
Becoming A Graduate Student

A QUESTION OF MOTIVATION

The most fundamental question someone can ask himself about post-graduate education is: Why go to graduate school? Because graduate education offers more specialized training requiring a greater effort than any previous academic schooling for an extended period of time, students must understand why they want to go on with their studies. Although this question is a favorite with counselors and although it sounds trite, it needs to be discussed because a large number of students do not know why they continue their education. Many fail to complete their graduate programs because they are disillusioned with courses; only a surprisingly low number find they cannot financially afford to finish their studies. For some, graduate school is boring, a routine they fall into with little hope of escape. Yet these doldrums can be avoided.

A great deal of motivation goes far to ensure that a student will complete his graduate education, whether for an M.A. or for a Ph.D. If you decide to go simply because your parents want or expect you to, count on facing a serious problem during the first year of school when you have to make fundamental decisions regarding subject specialization, research, and financing. In short, your parents' or teachers' wishes should not be the main consideration in deciding on graduate school. Consult with them; but make up your own mind about why you want to go on with schooling.

4

Becoming
A Graduate
Student

Others attend graduate schools simply because they did well as undergraduates or because they received some grant offers. These students usually feel that they need to delay going out into the world to look for a job. This attitude is more common among students than many educators will admit. Tragically, people who use this excuse feel that one, two, three, or more years in school will give them time to discover themselves and to decide what career to go into. The fact of the matter is, however, that there is little time in graduate school for such contemplation. You will be too busy reading in the library or being buried under a mountain of class presentations or lab reports to discover yourself. Such speculations about the future are better suited to the undergraduate, who has more time. Those who have done well in the past may really be continuing because they seek the security of being able to practice their profession—that of the student. Of course, some students come to graduate school vaguely knowing that they want to work in one area and then discover an exciting professor or program in another area and switch. But do not count on this to happen. If you honestly do not have precise objectives in mind, then at least have some broad general ideas; otherwise, you will waste time and energy taking courses which may, in the long run, not help you to complete the requirements of some specific program.

Another motivation that guides students is their desire to achieve a well-rounded, final polish to their undergraduate education by taking one or two years of graduate courses, culminating in an M.A. degree. This may or may not be the case, depending on what fields of study are involved. Some programs do not lend themselves to a generalized education; others do, such as an M.A. in American Studies. One way to check whether or not a specific program will satisfy the urge for a broad education is to study the number and types of courses offered within a department. See if minor fields can be taken in other areas. Ask someone who either teaches or is a student in the particular department if the program is narrow in scope. You will never know for sure until you actually take courses in the department; but it is possible to obtain some idea of what to expect in advance. Keep in mind that, as a whole, graduate education does not lend itself to broadness.

In fact, today, specialization is the name of the game. The more graduate education you receive, the narrower your studies will become as you are pushed into more and more restricted fields of study. As is the case at the undergraduate level, the more you learn, the more limited the scope of your courses tends to be. For example, an undergraduate biology major could, in graduate school, major in genetics and explore minor fields in biophysics and morphology. Consequently, you have to be very careful about choosing schools if breadth of program is a feature you want.

Usually however, the majority of students go to graduate school with some idea of what they want out of school. Although most of them will change some or all of their preconceptions, they at least have an advantage in feeling secure in the knowledge that they work with a purpose. Having a goal to motivate you cannot be overemphasized. In the first year of graduate school, you will work hard to establish a reputation with your peers and professors and to make sure that you meet the requirements of your classes. Self-doubts and lack of confidence can badly hurt your performance. If a student comes to graduate school with the intention of becoming a professor, for example, then he or she must earn a Ph.D. in order to be an academician. Knowing this, a student can work much better than one who simply likes the idea of having several degrees hanging on an office wall. Graduate school is hard work and you must have good reasons for being there: It is as simple as that!

A further word needs to be said about changing motivation. Although, graduate students do not modify their views about what they major in as often as undergraduates, they are still subject to new influences and ideas. Since most programs have major and minor fields at the M.A. and Ph.D. levels, it is not too uncommon for students to switch fields around within a department or even to add one from outside the department. Chapter Three will explain more about what is involved, but it is important to stress that one should not come to graduate school with a closed mind on all areas of study. Invariably, as one gains in understanding about the department and about its career outlets, one will make changes in his or her areas of study. Complete jumps from one department to another for a major are not common, but they are not rare either. Sometimes, students earn an M.A. in one field and then enroll in a Ph.D. program in another. Such a move can be effected without great hardships on the student. It is difficult, however, to switch from a social science to a natural science program or vice versa. This kind of

5
––––––––––––––
Becoming
A Graduate
Student

about face switch should not be anticipated by an undergraduate unless he or she has had extensive course work in the other field. Often, the real changes in what one studies will simply be reflected in the types of courses taken within a department.

PICKING A GRADUATE SCHOOL

Choosing a graduate school to attend is much like selecting an undergraduate college: You do the best you can and hope your choice is a good one. There is no perfect system for picking an ideal university. However, with considerable care, the chances of disappointment can be reduced. First, you need to decide whether you just want to earn an M.A. or whether you want to go through the Ph.D. program. Second, you must choose a field. Third, you need to determine whether you want a private or public university, a small or large one, taking into consideration tuition costs for in-state and out-of-state students. Make up your mind on whether you want to stay in one geographical area or move to another. Once some decisions regarding these points have been made, then more academic considerations can be taken into account.

When you apply to a university for a specific graduate program, you are really asking to be admitted into one department rather than to the university. Although your preliminary contacts and your final letter of acceptance will come from the university's office of admissions, one department will decide your fate. Consequently, most of your study of a university should be centered around the offerings of one department and on its peculiarities.

Initial information can be gained by talking to your undergraduate professors and asking them to make suggestions regarding universities that may have the kind of programs suitable to your tastes. Caution: Many professors teaching in colleges have been out of graduate school so long that their ideas on which departments at what universities are good and bad may be outdated. Therefore, view their advice both with respect and with some doubt. As a rule, discount your family's and friends' advice about a certain university or department since they generally have hearsay knowledge rather than current, accurate information about specific programs. For information go to professors, graduate students, and publications issued by professional or educational institutes designed for your purposes. One excellent guide for what departments offer is the American Council on Education's *A Guide to Graduate Study: Programs Leading to the Ph.D. Degree*, which is periodically updated. This excellent volume summarizes the catalogue contents of about 250 universities by departments. Like any detailed guide, it may become quickly outdated since costs of education go up, course offerings change, and professors move from one school to another. But this is a weakness that cannot be remedied and just has to be kept in mind.

The next step is to write to a few graduate schools which are of interest to you, perhaps up to one dozen, asking that they send you their graduate school catalogue and application forms. In your letters, emphasize that you want the graduate bulletin; otherwise, they will send the undergraduate catalogue. Then hope that, out of these dozen or so catalogues, you will find six universities at which to apply for admission. There is no use in applying to more because if your undergraduate record is good you will probably be accepted by more than one out of the six, and bothering with even a few can be expensive. Application fees range from $15 to $50, so even applying to six schools will cost quite a bit of money. Pick one dream school which you would love to attend but which may not accept you—but you never know; then apply at the same time to one you believe will take you—this is your insurance. For the rest, select universities you could attend and which would, in your opinion, accept you.

Between the time you begin to receive catalogues and the time when you file your applications, write the department heads to express your interest in their programs and to ask for details. Virtually all of them have a brochure or booklet describing the specific entrance requirements of the department, the courses offered and the professors who teach them, and what one must go through to earn a M.A. and Ph.D. Usually these bulletins shy away from discussing financial assistance; but some general idea about assistantships, fellowships, and loans can be gleaned from the general graduate catalogue. This initial, polite contact will call attention to your name early in the application process. Also, the brochures can be helpful in picking a program.

Reading the graduate school catalogue and the departmental pamphlet can be an almost meaningless exercise if not done properly. Universities hate to say anything specific in their catalogues; once in graduate school, you will find out that many programs are highly negotiable. They can be tailor-made to suit one person or they can be subject to the whim of a professor or administrator. Consequently, catalogues have to be read for certain types of information. Following are a few hints about what to search for in a bulletin.

1. Read the section on the department, looking for information regarding how many quarter or semester hours are required for both the M.A. and Ph.D. and whether a thesis is required for the M.A. Compare catalogues on these points, since they vary greatly. You may find that in one school you can earn an M.A. in nine months whereas in another it takes twice as long. If you have a rough idea of what you would like to major in within a department, check to make sure that such a field is offered and that it is backed by a series of courses taught by several professors. The more courses and professors listed in your area, the more flexibility you will have in choosing what to study and—more important—under whom. Do not, for example, pick a department that offers no courses in your area, hoping that you can convince your professors to develop a program especially for you. The same applies to minor fields. Since you probably have little idea about minor areas at this point, look for the school offering the largest number of areas or for the school offering several areas which are supported by an extensive number of courses and professors.

2. Notice the ranks of professors and where they earned their Ph.D.s. For graduate education, lean toward a department staffed with a large number of associate and full professors. If the number of full professors is less than one-third, be wary, because the full professors are usually the people who direct dissertation research and who are the most experienced instructors. Also, in the academic world, who you study under (as well as where) is often more important than the quality of the instruction. Although this statement may seem peculiar, it is nevertheless a fact of life. Chances are that a full professor has a better reputation within his profession than a more junior colleague. In all probability, a senior professor will be more able than a junior instructor to help you find a job later. This rule does not hold true in all cases, as

you will find out in graduate school; but if you know very little about a department, this suggestion can help. Many students have found it useful to ask an undergraduate professor to identify the more famous members of a prospective graduate department. If there is a renowned scholar in the department, one of your professors should be able to recognize the name; and, consequently, this can give you some idea of the possible reputation of the department. A famous name indicates that at least one member of the department is a productive scholar; and, since much of graduate school is research oriented, it also suggests that one member may be able to assist you in your future academic development.

3. Read the brief description of the library carefully. How many books it has is not as important as the number in your area of specialization. Note any special collections that could be of use to you. The same rule applies regarding scientific equipment, or—if you are a physical education major—the sports facilities. Check whether the library participates in inter-library loan (more on that later), does microfilming, and is a depository for government publications. Almost every graduate student will need these services and sources at one time or another. No matter what your area is, make sure the university has adequate facilities which will guarantee a suitable educational experience.

4. Examine what the catalogue says about in-state and out-of-state tuition costs and other required fees. If they look competitive with the other schools you are interested in, then write the Registrar for updated lists of fees. Tuition expenses have risen sharply each year for the past several and will probably continue to do so, outdating catalogue financial statements. Once you have chosen a school, write them again for a statement on expenses about one month before you arrive on campus, because the odds are that the fees have gone up. Generally, tuition costs are raised between June and September. Other fees are usually increased during the same period, but fees can be subject to change throughout the school year. Since tuition hikes can sometimes be large, it is important to keep abreast of these changes in order to avoid unexpected shocks.

A further word should be added about expenses at this point. If you can prove you were a resident of the state your chosen university is in for one year ending a week or even twenty-four hours before your second year of school, you can save on that fall's tuition expenses. As a rule, state universities charge over $100 more per quarter or semester for out-or-state students, as do some private universities. Therefore, find out how to become a resident of the state in which the university is located. Usually, one of the professors can tell you, or you can call up the local court house. Often a student must live in the state for twelve months before he or she can become a resident, which is usually confirmed by submitting proof of local domicile. This can be done by showing canceled checks for rent, a driver's license from the state, or a statement from the department saying you have been there one year. Since residency requirements vary in each state, ideally they should be checked out before arriving on campus in case a statement of domicile has to be filled out. Of course, if you plan to attend graduate school in the state in which you already live, you do not have to worry about citizenship: You already have it.

Besides the catalogue, your other major source of information is the department. Once you have asked for its brochure, most of your correspondence will be with the department. Your application will be on file there and a committee of professors will gather around a conference table one afternoon and decide whether or not to admit you. So if you have any questions to ask about the program, write the department. It never hurts to generate a little bit of paper work since it makes your name and record familiar to them before a decision is made on your application. But do not overdo it. Two or three thoughtfully written letters regarding the program and describing what you want to do will not only help you but will also help to guide the faculty in their decision. The more information they have on you, the more you appear to them as a person rather than a name. This may make the difference between an acceptance and a rejection. During the selection period, if you know a professor or a graduate student in the department, write them asking that they put in a good word for you. If your undergraduate major professor knows anyone, have him or her do some campaigning as well.

Students often write departments about the availability of assistantships and fellowships. Provision is usually made on the formal application form for a person to indicate whether he or she would like to be considered for aid during his first year in school. Unless your undergraduate record is outstanding, it would not be advisable to say you will not attend without financial aid. Plan on paying your way in full the first quarter, semester, or year (if possible), because a committee would be reluctant to give aid to a less than outstanding student for fear of throwing away money on someone who might not last in graduate school. Many who have good but not brilliant undergraduate records will receive aid once they come to the university and prove they can survive the program. Since favoritism is often a guiding factor in who is awarded financial aid, once you are on campus you can do the necessary crusading. If you arrive on campus and find that someone who had been given aid did not turn up in September, you could conceivably be his or her financial aid replacement by early October. And you will not have to risk being turned down because you were not good enough to be given aid sight unseen.

The application procedure itself is much the same as that for undergraduate schools. There are the usual long formal application forms which have to be filled out and the essay to write on why you want this particular school and on what your plans are for the future. The application itself is simple enough—you fill in the blanks with whatever information they want using a typewriter. The essay is more ticklish and has to be a carefully prepared paper, because the department will read it both for content and for command of the English language. You should tell the department about what you hope to achieve in graduate school; whether you are going after an M.A., a Ph.D., or both; what your professional aspirations are; and how you specifically plan to use the education you receive. Often they want some self-analysis concerning your character, personality, and motivation. Write the best essay you can, even though you do not really know what you hope to achieve in graduate school. Take what you think is a polished paper to your major professor and have him or her critique it for both style and content. Then rewrite it before copying or typing it on the back of the application form. Usually you have space for an essay of between five hundred and one thousand words: Keep within this limit; no one wants to read your autobiography yet.

Most graduate schools will require that you take the Graduate Record Examination (known as the GRE), the Miller Analogies Test (MAT), or similar examinations. Most popular is the GRE, which is set up much like college boards—except that it is harder. The morning portion lasts three hours and tests general aptitude, both verbally and mathematically, while the afternoon part deals with your major field and is also three hours long. Both are treated as separate exams and must be applied for as two tests. They are usually taken in the fall or winter of your senior year. The MAT test is taken at the same time and only takes fifty minutes. Both are given in many colleges and universities throughout the country. For MAT information and application forms, write the Psychological Corporation at 304 East 45th Street, New York, New York 10017. For the GRE, usually given in November, January, March, April, and July, write the Educational Testing Service, Box 955, Princeton, New Jersey 08540— if you live in the eastern part of the United States. If you live in the western part of the country address your inquiry to 1947 Center Street, Berkeley, California 94704. Check with the department you are applying to in order to determine if you have to take the advanced part of the GRE dealing with your major field; if you do not have to, save yourself some work. Whether you take the GRE or MAT, you must apply for them about six weeks or more in advance of the test date.

Although commercial testing services argue that you cannot study adequately for their exams, graduate students will tell you that it helps to make some preparations. Your college bookstore will undoubtedly have several large paperbacks designed to help you prepare for these tests. Usually they give examples of the questions asked and a long list of obscure vocabulary words—which invariably turn up on the exams. Perhaps the best thing to do would be first, to learn as many of the words as possible, both their spelling and meaning. This often means working with about one thousand words. Second, find a general high school math book and refresh your memory about basic algebra, geometry, and old-fashioned mathematical word problems. For the advanced test, read one or more good general survey textbooks in your field, preferably those recommended by your major professor. Again, the object is just to refresh your memory about a large number of facts.

How important a score is to your admission depends on the department. Some schools have a minimum score you must achieve to be considered for admission; others do not. A few universities will provisionally admit to graduate school students who have never taken these tests, with the understanding that this requirement will be met within a few months. If the student does poorly on these tests and yet has done well in his courses, the department may overlook the weak point. Usually, the catalogue and the departmental brochure will have statements regarding their testing policies. Like anything else in your application, a bad score would probably hurt your chances for admission while a good score, even if you did not need it, certainly could not.

All applicants are required to submit letters of recommendation, which are sent to the department. As an undergraduate, you probably had letters written by neighbors, teachers, and your minister. For graduate school, have three or four (the number varies) professors or employers write the letters. If you know enough professors within your major field who you feel will write favorable comments, better to have them than one or two from outside your major. The only general exception might be to have a teacher who instructed you in your minor to write a letter also. Follow up on your request for letters to make sure they were sent because it is imperative to have all your grades, application forms, letters, and other documentation in *before* the deadline date set by the university. Failure to do so may cost you an acceptance letter, and there is simply no excuse for such sloppy performance. Also make sure that your college forwards your transcripts. Keep a separate folder for each university you are applying to with a list of things to be done; and as they are completed, check them off. In this way you can keep track of a lot of paper work.

Because competition to get into graduate school is rough, pull every string you have. If your grandfather built a dorm at the school, ask him to write the university, or have someone tactfully remind the school of the fact—but do not inform the department. It is better that a dean call the chairman to remind him of the splendid building your grandfather built. The hint may be sufficient. Have any friends who are either teaching or attending classes within the department put in a good word for you. If you never knew anything about politics before you went to graduate school, this may be a good time to start practicing this ancient trade.

If you are rejected by a school, hope that the other five will heal your wounded ego. The world is not lost yet. If you are accepted by several and decide which one to attend, write the others to tell them politely that you will not be able to attend their fine schools. At the same time, write both to the Registrar and to the chairman of the department in the school you did choose, telling them that you will be attending classes. Ask the chairman about when you should be on campus, about preregistration for courses, and whether an advisor could be assigned to you with whom you could communicate, if need be, before classes start. If you are assigned an advisor, write him or her explaining who you are, when you will arrive in town, and something about what you would like to know regarding the program. Courtesies of this nature can ingratiate you a little before you even arrive at the university and can help your image once registration is over and classes start.

PREPARING FOR GRADUATE WORK

If you are still an undergraduate, there is time left to prepare even more fully for graduate work. One of the reasons why many students cannot succeed in graduate school is that they are unprepared for what lies ahead. This has nothing to do with brains or good grades, it is just that some students do not have the background necessary to complete graduate studies. However, this problem can be remedied in part with some effort on the part of the student.

The further you go in your studies, the more you will become aware that academic work is like an inverted ice cream cone. As an undergraduate, your education is the product of work done in many departments. In graduate school, your education is often the result of studies done in one department, possibly two. The higher up you go in education, the narrower the work becomes and the less time you have available to fill gaps in related fields. Consequently, undergraduates should think in terms of gaining as broad an education at the college level as possible. Specialization will come later at the M.A. and Ph.D. levels. It is foolish to specialize too early other than to pick a major, because you cheat yourself out of auxiliary courses of possible interest. Besides the personal satisfaction of studying in many fields, there is the more immediate problem of the GRE, which will test a wide spectrum of information in the humanities and in the social and natural sciences. A person with a broad educational background will probably do better than the student who has taken all of his electives in his major field.

Do not avoid language study as an undergraduate. Today, many students still agitate for the elimination of all language requirements for the B.A. Although it is not our purpose to pass judgment on such a proposal, this issue can have serious implications for all students wishing to attend graduate school. If you think you will ever go to graduate school, then you will probably have one or possibly two language translating tests to pass. Do not count on your more energetic reforming friends to convince your university to eliminate the language requirements for graduate degrees. Most departments will not even discuss the issue. If you study one language for two years as an undergraduate, when you have more time to spend on the subject, you will not have to waste time and effort taking courses in graduate school in order to pass your first language test. If you already know a second language as a freshman, it might be a good idea to study a third one just in case you need it in graduate school.

Most graduates will tell you that learning a language at the undergraduate level is far less painful than learning it later. As an undergraduate, you are accustomed to studying diverse subjects, and you do not get into the mental habit of saying, as do many graduate students: "I am not interested in anything not directly in my field." In graduate school, you will probably hate the language requirement and will wish you had taken one in college so that you can pass over the first language hurdle. If you are a junior or senior and lack any language preparation, take some language, even if it is only for a quarter or a semester. This is at least some preparation for your future requirements. It would be difficult to overemphasize what a major stumbling block languages can be for graduate students. They must be taken seriously. In graduate school, it is simply too easy to say: "I'll study my French tomorrow, I have to read this important book tonight." Avoid a headache and lost time—study a language.

Another way to prepare for graduate work is to use your electives wisely, taking courses outside of your major but in related fields. For example, an American history major should consider the wisdom of taking a junior level course in American literature and studying American government, art, or drama. A biology major should take courses in chemistry, physics, and math which are not required. It is also useful to take a course in writing, since there will be reports to work on in graduate school.

Do not shy away from taking courses calling for a lot of writing. Too many people come to graduate school unable to compose a good sentence, and yet professors expect students to write with some degree of polish. Although grammar courses could help writing style, the best teacher is practice. Register for classes in which you have to write research papers, essays, and book reviews. It is also easy to ask professors in such courses to help you with your style, to point out your mistakes, and to suggest improvements. Even though you will receive a great deal of individual attention concerning your writing style from your professors in graduate school, an atrocious writer will be given up for lost and a fairly good one will receive help: Professors want to feel that their efforts are not totally wasted. Although they would be the first to deny such a statement, it is nonetheless true, so help yourself by taking a writing course. In some graduate courses, grades are based solely on term papers. Think of that next time you contemplate ducking out of a class because of a paper. And there is another factor to consider: A good undergraduate paper can often be converted into a graduate essay with little effort.

In regard to grades, most graduate schools require, as a bare minimum, at least a B average in the undergraduate major and something close to a B for an overall record. The top schools in the country demand even higher standards; some ask for a 3.8 overall and a 4.0 in the major. Graduate schools today have more applicants than ever before and at a time when they are reluctant to expand their programs, either because of budgetary problems or because they cannot find jobs for their graduates. Consequently, competition to get into graduate school is increasing. It is especially important to earn the highest possible grades in the major. Schools can forgive a disastrous freshman year, but a C or D in an important course in the major taken during the junior or senior year will not pass unnoticed. If your school has honor societies, join these in order to accent your good marks.

If you like participating in many campus activities, go right ahead and satisfy this drive as much as possible while you are an undergraduate—provided that your grades do not suffer. As a graduate student, this phase of your academic life may come to an end because your studies will claim most of your time. A great number of extracurricular affairs in graduate school can be fatal. In picking their graduate students, most departments are not concerned with your various extracurricular activities, except for whatever positions of leadership you have held within the student government, in scholastic societies, or in your previous career. They are interested in tracing leadership qualities and in determining whether you are a team worker; but they have little desire to read a long list of clubs to which you belong. Ideally, you want a few extracurricular items on your record to prove that you did not live in a closet for four years.

As an undergraduate, develop the habit of reading a great deal—more than is required in your classes. Do it both in your major field and in other areas. This helps to broaden one's views. This may be the best opportunity you will ever have to read books having absolutely nothing to do with your work, so take advantage of your time. You do have the problem of disciplining your mind, and increasing your reading speed, and becoming used to sitting for several hours each day concentrating on one subject. This is excellent preparation for graduate work. If you should be assigned a book later which you happened to have read as an undergraduate, you may not need to read it again. Saving a few hours this way is vital, since you never have enough time for all your work.

It would be a good idea to begin immediately to develop close relationships with your professors, especially those in your major field. This is a relatively easy thing to do at a small college but is far more difficult at a large school. Two things should be kept in mind. First, by talking to a professor more often than just to complain about a grade, you learn things about your field and about possible job outlets which you may not be exposed to in class. At the same time, you will have an opportunity to discuss these issues on a one to one basis. Since you will be doing a great deal of this in graduate school, it never hurts to start early—and such rap sessions can be both informative and fun. Second, your professors have an opportunity to know you and to know what your mind is like. This is important to them, because when the time comes to write letters of recommendation—either for graduate schools or for jobs—they will be able to do more than just discuss a name and grades. People who know you will probably be more likely to write friendly, understanding letters of recommendation, which are always read with great interest by the next department you apply to. Also, a professor will usually be more willing to use influence to ensure the acceptance of a student he or she knows than he or she might be for someone with whom he or she only has a passing acquaintance.

When you begin to think you might want to go to graduate school, do some research concerning what that involves in terms of years, courses, programs, and money. Talk to your professors and to your friends in graduate school—and, of course, buy this book. If you do your research well, there should be few rude shocks once you arrive at your new campus.

Graduate programs are rapidly undergoing changes. Advanced degrees are now being offered in fields that did not exist five years ago. As a result, many employers are asking that their more technical jobs be filled with people who have had a graduate education of some sort. It is imperative to find out while you are an undergraduate what programs exist in the fields you might possibly want to work with in order to plan far in advance for the right kind of graduate work backed by the proper undergraduate preparation. Although many students would argue that they do not know what they will be doing in several years, it never hurts to explore your possibilities.

GRADUATE PROGRAMS: THE M.A. AND PH.D.

Subsequent chapters will assume that you have arrived in graduate school; but, since they develop some idea of what it means to be a graduate student, they can be read for profit by undergraduates as well.

Many students make the decision to go on to graduate school without really knowing anything about advanced programs. Although a variety of graduate degrees can be earned, there are essentially two that are universal and that form the core of any graduate program: the Master of Arts and the Doctorate of Philosophy, more commonly called the M.A. (and its variant, the Master of Science) and the Ph.D. The superior of the two is the doctorate, which is considered the highest degree a university can award. Although in the past generation there has been a boom in education, both in terms of programs offered and students enrolled, M.A. and Ph.D. programs have essentially retained fun-

18

—————

*Becoming
A Graduate
Student*

damental characteristics which are found in virtually all graduate schools. It should be kept in mind that the description given below of these programs is a generalized one at best and that it is subject to qualifications by every department in the country.

The M.A., or Master of Arts, and its science counterpart, the Master of Science, (M.S.), has the general purpose of providing both an introduction to the scholarship of a given field and exposure to further study in one area. Like the B.A. degree program, it is—to a great extent, but not completely—course-oriented. Usually, a student will be required to take a certain number of credit hours leading to the M.A., taking from one to two years, with the average falling somewhere in between, to complete the program. One registers for classes which are basically an extension of what is studied by undergraduates, only in greater depth. Also, practical experience working in the field is stressed more than at the undergraduate level. Hence the social worker will actually do social work while enrolled in an M.A. program; the chemistry major will spend more hours working in a laboratory than he ever thought possible; and the drama major will act in more plays than he or she has in the past.

While being exposed to research or new techniques currently being developed by his or her professors or fellow graduate students, the pupil will be expected to make an attempt at offering new ideas and research in unchartered waters. Although catalogues and departmental bulletins will state in glowing terms that graduate work is essentially research-minded, do not be fooled. When it comes to studying, an M.A. student is treated only a little better than an undergraduate. You are expected to absorb large quantities of facts and to be able to regurgitate them on your exams—just the way your professors presented them to you. In practice, a graduate student is sometimes required to learn more about a field in less time than are undergraduates. Soaking up facts such as names and dates is a sad fact of life. Creativity is not encouraged during the first year of graduate work; that comes later.

Built into many M.A. programs is a language requirement, especially in the more traditional fields, such as history, political science, English, physics, and chemistry, to name a few. This is less so in some of the newer areas: physical education, criminol-

19
―――――――
*Becoming
A Graduate
Student*

ogy, modern dance, and social welfare. But again, the requirement varies with departments. One school insists upon language for the M.A. while the next does not. What the requirement means is that a student must be able to pass an examination which proves that he or she can do research in a foreign language. This stipulation can usually be met in a number of ways. One may sometimes be allowed to submit B or A grade averages for two or more years of undergraduate language study. Another is to take a certain number of hours in a language while in graduate school.

A more popular measure with most schools is simply to administer an exam through the appropriate language department, although some departments do the job themselves. The test often consists of giving a student a passage in a foreign language book and asking that 300 or more words be translated into coherent English within an hour. Often, a student is allowed to use verb wheels and dictionaries. Other departments will require that a test prepared by the Educational Testing Service at Princeton (the GRE people again) be given. This test is given at all universities four times a year or more. If you have a choice, pick the department's own exam. It is easier than the Princeton test because the latter will ask questions about grammar, will have you provide specific data, and will not permit the use of a dictionary. The test can be difficult, especially for someone who does not do well on multiple choice exams. When allowed the use of a dictionary, many people feel they can pass without knowing too much about the language.

For the student who comes to graduate school with little or no language background, most universities give noncredit courses in all the major languages which are geared toward the translation tests. Attendance in these classes for six months is often sufficient for one to be able to pass the test. When you arrive on campus, check with the other graduate students in your department on what the language requirements are and about how they have solved that problem. You may find that a particular French teacher will pass virtually everyone who takes the test provided that he or she attends one of her classes regularly. Or you may discover that one language test is far easier on a given campus than at another. The special courses carry no letter grade and count only as credit hours. The exams, usually given once each quarter or semester, are on a pass/fail basis and can usually be taken as many times as you wish.

Many students put off satisfying their language requirements for the M.A. and Ph.D. to the last minute only to find they are in serious trouble because they lack the ability to pass the necessary tests. Experience shows that the student who immediately tries to pass the exam during the first or second quarter on campus, using undergraduate language training, is far better off than a friend who faces the problem after all the M.A. course work is out of the way. If you delay taking the exam, you may find that you have to study a language long after you have finished your degree requirements. If you try the test early and fail it, you can still prepare for a rematch while you are taking your degree courses. If you pass it the first time, as many people do, then the problem is behind you. It is surprising how many students you meet who cannot finish a degree simply because of the language requirement. It is not an impossible obstacle, but it ought to be faced early. Should you pass the exam shortly after starting graduate work and you feel that you might continue on for a Ph.D., attend classes for a new language. For the more advanced degree, you will have to pass a second exam in a different language in order to offer reading knowledge in two languages, a standard requirement in many doctoral programs.

Besides courses and a language requirement, many M.A. programs have a thesis. This is a research project running in typed length anywhere from twenty-five pages to two hundred; it does not necessarily need to reflect original research. Where the thesis is required, its purpose is to demonstrate that the student has some research and writing abilities. The time required to prepare a thesis varies with each student. Some will crank it out in a month, while others will slave over the project for a year. Many master's programs do not require a thesis and instead substitute additional courses to be taken. This practice is becoming more widespread each year. For example, in many universities a student can substitute a skill for a language requirement, for example, statistics courses in computer analysis. Two or more courses may substitute for the thesis requirement. Again, this varies with each department. Taking several extra courses instead of the thesis is often less work, but one must decide whether that is a wise decision to make.

Generally speaking, if you plan to continue on for a Ph.D. and afterwards apply for a teaching job, especially at a college or university, it would probably be a good idea to write a thesis, particularly if it can be done on a topic suitable for a dissertation. This shows that you can do research, allows you indirectly to start on a dissertation project, and gives the faculty some indication of your scholarly potential. More important, however, it provides you with an opportunity to practice writing, since you probably went through college with few written assignments. If you came from a large undergraduate school, your professors were probably too lazy to assign term papers to monster classes; and if you attended a small college, you still may have had little writing experience. By writing a thesis you will be forced to rewrite material several times for your major professor who, in turn, may show you line by line how to improve your style.

If you view the M.A. as a terminal degree and plan to work either outside the degree area or in a less scholarly position, taking courses instead of writing a thesis may be the right decision to make. In some programs, thesis requirements can be fulfilled simply by submitting one or more term papers written for graduate courses to the department as proof of your scholarship. These variations on the thesis have to be explored by you during the first several months on campus, both with professors and with fellow students, in order to decide on your best option.

The one other requirement which appears in most M.A. programs is a comprehensive examination of all that the student has studied. This is actually taken at the end of the program, either before or after the thesis has been completed. The exam may be based on given field(s), irrespective of the courses you have taken, or solely on the classes you have attended. It may be a written exam, an oral test given by a group of professors, or a combination of the two. When a thesis is presented, there is usually a thesis defense as well. This consists of an hour or two of oral questioning by a committee of professors who have read your paper. It is not as bad as it may appear, because the questions are usually the type that one might hear asked of an author on a TV talk show. And since you are temporarily an expert on the particular topic involved, you should be able to answer all questions without too much difficulty. The defense is more of a ritual than anything else and can be an enjoyable experience. Before undergoing the definse, you will have long ago learned how your committee acts on these tests and will be prepared for any quirks that pop up.

Some mention has to be made about major professors and committees. Upon starting graduate work, every student is assigned an advisor who is responsible for making sure that he or she satisfies all the degree requirements. The advisor is there to answer the thousand and one questions you will have. As soon as you have picked a specialization, then the professor in charge of that field becomes your major professor and advisor. He or she is in fact your intellectual parent, your mentor. You will write your thesis for this professor, you will probably take courses from him or her, and you will seek his or her advice on academic matters. Usually, the relationship between student and major professor develops into a mutual admiration society. Your professor often fights the in-house battles for your grants and defends you against any nasty professor who dislikes you. Your major professor is an ally as well as a teacher. You will also have a committee composed of from two to six teachers with whom you have usually studied. They read your thesis, pass judgment on it, and administer your comprehensive examination. In a lesser sense, these individuals can also be considered allies, that is, unless there are serious personality clashes between you and a committee member.

The Ph.D. program has essentially the same format as the M.A. schedule, except that there is more of it. Many say that "Ph.D." stands for "Piled higher and Deeper," which is more truth than fiction. The number of courses taken is usually the same as for the master's degree—or twice the number if the student has had no previous graduate work. Instead of one language requirement, there are now two; a committee is usually two or three professors larger than before; comprehensive examinations (better known as comps) last longer; and then there is the dissertation. Besides these superficial similarities, there are some fundamental differences.

After a student has completed the M.A. and chooses to continue for the Ph.D. degree (which may take between two and five years beyond the master's), he or she will have to take a preliminary examination (prelim) early in the new program in order to demonstrate some factual knowledge in the doctoral area. The prelim is ordinarily an oral examination in which the professors huddle around an impressive conference table and ask the student questions for an hour or two. The pupil who passes is permitted to continue taking courses toward the degree. The classes themselves begin to change; you take fewer lecture courses and you do more reading and research. Essentially, the Ph.D. program today still continues to be a research degree, far more than the M.A. The student sharpens his or her intellectual capacities, learns to read with a discriminating mind, and continues to practice writing skills. The dissertation topic must be original and a contribution to knowledge. The time required to do the research and writing is far more than that required for a thesis; it may take years, with extensive travel or long hours in a laboratory or archive. After classes are completed but before the dissertation is written, comprehensive examinations taking from one to two weeks to complete cap the program. Not only is the student required to have factual knowledge about more fields than for the M.A., but he or she must also be familiar with the bibliography of these fields. In numerous departments, a student has to understand, in general terms, what topics have not been studied in the past. A student thus has to appreciate subjects that are in need of research which are currently not being examined by someone else.

The emphasis at the doctoral level is on training professors and scholars. Consequently, students will be expected to lecture, either in the courses they take or in classes which they teach. More term paper writing faces them as well. In practice, the extra writing load may hardly be discernable from that at the M.A. level, and most students question the originality of much of their work.

Essentially, the Ph.D. program is divided into two parts. The first is the period spent taking courses and passing language examinations and comps. Once these requirements are completed, the student is an A.B.D., All But Degree. Some universities will issue a diploma based on just this amount of work and call it a Master of Philosophy or a Doctor of Arts. But normally the student is labeled an A.B.D., neither fish nor fowl. The second is the period of research and writing the dissertation and is the time that may be as long or longer than the first half. The minimum amount of time most universities like a student to spend on the dissertation is one year. This period is not pock-marked by classes or by other academic requirements, although the student may do some teaching or other work in order to ward off starvation. At the completion of the research, a committee reads the drafts of the dissertation text just as they do for the thesis. Once this reading is completed, an oral examination is given by the committee. As with the thesis defense, this oral examination is more of a ritual than a test, since the student usually knows more about the topic than do any of the faculty members.

DIFFERENCES BETWEEN UNDERGRADUATE AND GRADUATE PROGRAMS

There are some interesting contrasts between undergraduate and graduate education that you should know. As a group, your peers are good students who have excellent undergraduate records. They also display far more interest in their subject than did your undergraduate friends. Coupled with this concern is their greater age, accounting for a greater sense of responsibility for their studies. Most graduates are required to read far more than undergraduates, and the older student can usually do this reading more quickly. Your research and writing are expected to be of superior quality. Because you will be doing more of this anyway, your skills will improve with time.

Courses change at the graduate level as well. Usually, classes tend to be on much narrower topics, and they are either of the lecture variety, such as undergraduates take, or seminars where students present class reports which their peers and professors then discuss. In some classes, students are simply assigned readings instead of listening to lectures; they then write book reviews or confer with professors regarding assignments. In any case, the student is expected to learn more factual and interpretative material than his or her junior associates, to have a deeper understanding about a field, and to be able to offer original or imaginative insights into an area in the form of comments, lectures, or papers.

Graduate schools approach the problem of grades slightly differently than do colleges. Although catalogues state that the grade spread A through F, with S (satisfactory) and U (unsatisfactory), holds for graduate students, in reality, the grades assigned are A, B, or C. In graduate school, a B means average and a C means failure. Most graduate schools require that you maintain at least a B average. In effect this is not difficult and is the same as telling an undergraduate that he or she must maintain a C average.

Professors willingly tend to give more As to graduate students on the assumption that graduates work better than undergraduates, which may not necessarily reflect the truth. Sometimes S or U grades can be issued, often for thesis and dissertation hours, occasionally for reading courses, and rarely for seminars. But as a rule, the A through C listing is used, since it gives a more precise statement about a student's performance.

Students spend more time in laboratories and in libraries than ever before. No doubt you have heard about how hard graduate students are made to study. The successful student will learn how much to study and when, much like undergraduates do; but the work load is still heavy. There are the problems of quickly digging deeply into a field and of building a reputation of excellence within a department. Both of these objectives call for a student to work very hard; this is especially so for the new students who have yet to learn what constitutes superior work. Most professors treat graduate students almost as junior colleagues rather than as students, and the longer one stays in graduate school the more obvious this becomes. One is treated as an adult and should act accordingly. You are expected to always go to your classes, to turn in papers and other assignments on time, and never to be absent from tests for exams. Failure to produce on time is a sin that is more noticed in a graduate student than in an undergraduate.

As an undergraduate, you could take a course, pass its exam, and then promptly forget everything you learned. In order to graduate, you merely needed to collect a certain number of hours, properly distributed among a variety of fields, and then turn those in for a sheepskin. Not so in graduate school. Because of the comprehensive examinations which have to be taken at the end of the course work in graduate school, you cannot afford to forget what you learned in a class; often you have to force yourself to continue your reading in specific course areas. Only after you have passed your comps can you efface the material from memory.

Because of comps, students are always trying to learn new material. Their private conversations often center around academic topics rather than the weather or sports. This feature of graduate life largely explains why graduates are real packrats:

They save their old class lectures, duplicate other sets of notes, and save bibliographies and books—all with the idea that these might come in handy while preparing for the exams. The comps' influence is thus in many ways the greatest difference between graduate education and college work.

Universities take less interest in the private living arrangements of its graduate students than in those of the undergraduates. Some schools have apartments on campus which students share; usually there are few or no rules governing student behavior. Facilities for married students are also common at many universities, but both kinds of on-campus living accommodations are so few in number that only a minority of graduate students can use them. You will usually have to establish your own living quarters in town, such as an apartment or a boarding house. The most a university will do is to provide lists of vacant apartments and rooms on request. Living off campus allows one far more freedom than ever before.

Another difference is cost. It is more expensive to be a graduate student than it is to be an undergraduate. Tuition is higher and so are book and lab fees. Housing and food tend to cost more since you live off campus and, because you are older, your standard of living changes to satisfy certain personal tastes. Expenses vary with students, but they may equal those of people working full time who are the same age. You might want to gauge your expenses with that idea in mind. Chapter Two discusses finances in greater detail.

DROPPING OUT OR TRANSFERRING IN GRADUATE SCHOOL

One problem facing many graduate students is how to leave school gracefully if they decide not to complete their degree programs. It is not too uncommon for fledgling graduates to become disillusioned or bored with graduate studies. Others decide to change major fields, while some cannot afford the costs. And in a few cases, students find that they are unable to do the work properly or that they have personality conflicts with their professors. Therefore, the question arises: How does one go about dropping out of school? The trick is to do this diplomatically, without hurting anyone's feelings. This way, you can still come back at some future date without a black mark against you.

Do not tell your advisor or major professor that you are leaving because of a personality clash. Avoid criticizing the program. Even if you feel it is bad, do not broadcast your views, even to fellow graduate students. Departments resemble small towns: In no time, everybody knows what everyone else is doing. You might argue that you need time to think about what you really want to study. Say that you sincerely wish to change fields, explaining the logic behind your decision. Why create bitter feelings when they can be avoided? If you are deeply into the program—say, one year—try to finish your M.A. so you will at least have some recognition for the hard work you did.

For students who wish to transfer to other departments or universities, tact and timing are essential. It is easier to transfer as an M.A. graduate than with a collection of graduate courses and no degree. Once you have done over fifty percent of the course work, it is very difficult to transfer to another department or university without a heavy loss in credits and time. Most schools require students to do at least fifty percent of their work on campus or to spend a certain period of time in residence irrespective of previous graduate work. Therefore, if you decide to transfer, do it very early—perhaps at the end of a quarter or semester, if possible—or immediately after you complete the M.A. Explain to your professors that your brief experience in school has suggested exactly what specialization you want—a specialization which is, unfortunately, not offered at this university—and that this forces you to move on to a school that has the courses you need. Professors can understand and readily accept this. Also, their cooperation and friendship are vital because they will usually be asked to comment on your academic performance for the next university to which you apply. Anything less than glowing letters of recommendation will make switching more difficult.

If you really cannot afford to continue on with your studies and the department or university has not seen fit to give you financial help, tell your professors that this is why you are dropping out. It is amazing how spare dollars in some scholarship fund appear all of a sudden out of nowhere. It is to a department's advantage to keep as many students as possible, because the more they have, the bigger their budget will be next year. If the department cannot raise funds for you, at least you can leave with their sympathy and understanding. And what is more important, you can come back in the future with little difficulty, and possibly with some financial aid.

Leaving in a wave of friendliness is simply good sense. But above all, you should make sure that you have no regrets about dropping out. Have no shame or self-doubts, because deserting a graduate program does not carry the same stigma that leaving an undergraduate school might. Consider your graduate work a useful experience to have gone through and move on to other activities.

2
Financing Graduate Studies

For several reasons, financing graduate study often proves to be a bigger problem than paying undergraduate expenses. Graduate work costs more. Tuition is higher and one has to buy more books. There is usually also the increased expense of living off campus. By the time they come to graduate school, many students are married and may even have children. Others are in their late twenties or early thirties and may have some reservations about running to their parents for school expenses. After having imposed on them for four years of undergraduate education, they may feel reluctant to ask for more funds. But the picture is not as gloomy as it appears. In fact, there are financial sources available for the graduate student that undergraduates would find difficult or impossible to tap. Perhaps the most common way to finance graduate school is by a combination of various methods. Essentially there are four fundamental sources of income for the student: the family, working, nonuniversity grants, and funds from the student's school.

FAMILY SOURCES

Some fortunate individuals can finance part or all of their graduate education through their own private means or by using family resources. Some go to parents or to a wealthy relative; some dig into a trust fund. A great many students do receive some form of help from their families. A more common formula used by couples is for one to work full-time while the other either works part-time or devotes an all-out effort to studies. This practice is so widespread that, in combination with some assistance from the university, one can be ensured of a fairly comfortable standard of living.

Upon your arrival at graduate school, you may hear stories about how a student married to a working wife got a divorce soon after he received his Ph.D. Although studies have been undertaken on this phenomenon, it should be pointed out that the stresses and strains of being married while in graduate school are sometimes exaggerated. Divorces among graduate students and recent degree recipients only reflect national trends. Although you will undoubtedly hear some professor comment on this problem, it is more mythical than real. Graduate schools do not cause divorces, people do. And do not think that an employed spouse will jeopardize your marriage, either. In fact, a working spouse will probably ensure your ability to finish school with fewer worries.

If a spouse works, it behooves the other to take on many of the household chores that otherwise would be left undone. Those attending school do not have to bow to the 9:00 to 5:00 god and consequently can take care of nonacademic matters which the working partner cannot perform. Domestic duties may perhaps be neglected if both are working, but a pattern of sharing the work should be developed early so that neither partner feels overtaxed. Although this may sound tangential to financing graduate school, it is nevertheless a problem that often comes up among married students. It is important to keep the breadwinner happy; otherwise, a major source of income could dry up!

WORKING OUTSIDE YOUR DEPARTMENT

Some students, both single and married, must work part- or full-time in order to finance their education, while others have found that they can earn enough money from summer jobs to carry them through the winter months. A few feel that they must work full-time and only take one course, while others try both a heavy work schedule and a full load of classes. Doing both full-time is considered a foolish move by most students, since your grades could suffer as a result. It would be better to work full-time and only have one course in which you do well than to take several classes and make poor marks. Many students are able to find part-time work while they go to school, and this seems to be one of the most practical formulas to try.

Part-time work is not difficult to find, especially if you are content with a mediocre salary. There are several good sources of information about such employment: the campus employment or placement office, which is well-informed about the local job market; city and town employment agencies; state employment agencies; and friends or professors. As a start, consult the university employment office. You might be able to find a job on campus which would eliminate the need to commute and which may be interesting work. Library science majors may find that there are job openings in the university library, business majors and higher education people may find slots in the administration, and natural science students often find federally funded research projects on campus in need of more personnel. Frequently, these various campus jobs pay slave wages—but they *are* jobs. Such positions are not usually listed by city and state employment agencies because universities like to save them for needy students. That is why you should consult the campus employment office.

If you work about fifteen hours a week, you can still be a full-time student. If you work more than that, you will be pushing your luck and you may possibly hurt your health. If you must work long hours, try finding a job related to your field or, even better, one where you are able to study. Premium on such a list are being a night watchman, a desk clerk at a local motel, a receptionist, or a babysitter. If you are a journalism major, run down to the local newspaper and find out if they have an opening: They may be looking for a reporter—or maybe only for a photo lab assistant—but try, anyway. A business major may be able to procure employment with some company in town and the ex-army medic may be able to obtain work in the emergency room of the local hospital.

The types of jobs students can find in a community are often limited only by a person's imagination. One could substitute teach; tutor undergraduates; type term papers; do part time social and recreational work; or be a sales clerk, waiter, waitress, or performer. If worse comes to worst, you can scrape bugs off windshields at the local truck stop between one and five A.M.; at least you would get the minimum hourly wage. Do not forget to contact libraries, research labs, government agencies, hospitals, bookstores, and independent campus organizations.

If you make things, there may well be a demand for your goods both on and off campus, depending on the quality of the work and your marketing abilities. Common along this line are leatherwork, knitting and jewelry. Local bazaars and boutiques, campus fairs, and local art shows often carry such products. If you paint or sculpt, your campus probably has several art shows a year where you could sell your wares.

More than undergraduates, graduate students with a flair for writing can make considerable sums of money with their skills, both through their own efforts or with the help of their professors. Writing short stories or articles for newspapers and magazines can be enjoyable work. It is not uncommon for a newspaper to pay $25 to $50 for an article, and magazines will pay even more. If you write, and if you do develop connections with a leading state newspaper, you might easily earn several hundred dollars a month at the cost of only a few hours of work per week. But you have to be good, and there is no way to find out unless you try.

The natural born salesman might sell magazines, brushes, encyclopedias, newspapers, Bibles, or pots and pans. Although this kind of work is usually unpopular because there is no steady income from it, you can resort to it if everything else fails. No matter how you solve your job problem, remember that you have to go out looking for employment: The jobs are there, despite the unemployment figures. The work may not pay well, but some money is better than none.

GRANTS AND FELLOWSHIPS

Approximately one-third of any given group of students in graduate school has some financial aid in the form of grants, fellowships, or assistantships. These various means can be long term, low interest loans from state and federal agencies, from the university, or from a bank. They can be outright lump sum grants or monthly payments from private institutions and foundations, universities, or government agencies. Some require work in return, usually for the university under the aegis of a department or professor or as a full-time paid employee for a certain length of time after graduation. There are many combinations of financial assistance available to students. Essentially, three major categories of grants exist which students can consider: funds covering academic work up to the completion of comps, funds supporting dissertation research only, and funds which finance all graduate work from start to finish.

In order to find out about these grants, consult your professors, stop by your campus scholarship and student aid offices, and look up one of a dozen published guides to grants. Grant catalogues can be found in student scholarship offices or in the reference section of the library, or they may be purchased very inexpensively in any decent bookstore. The bibliography at the end of this book lists a few of these catalogues. Since many grants change in stipulations and in quantity each year, always study the latest editions. Other excellent sources of information are graduate students within your department who have been grant recipients. Once you have found out about various financial sources, write for information concerning qualifications, applications, and the amounts of money involved.

The more famous of the available grants include the National Defense Education Act (N.D.E.A.), which is given by the United States Government and which may be used for almost all graduate work, and of course, the Woodrow Wilson Fellowships, which may cover all graduate work or be used just for dissertation research. Each branch of learning also has its coveted and not so coveted grants; these are listed in professional publications and are known to most of your professors. Foundations and other institutions periodically announce new fellowships which are soon listed in leading scholarly journals. You simply have to look at the latest issues of the top journals in your field in order to find out about new grants. As a matter of fact, journals are often the best source of information, especially regarding recently established grants which have not yet been listed in book length guides to scholarships.

UNIVERSITY AID

The university you plan to attend or in which you are enrolled has several sources of financial aid: Some are built into the annual budget and some arise from special funds earning interest for the university or for your department. These are listed either in special brochures published by the university or in the catalogue. Universities allocate a percentage of their yearly budgets for graduate assistantships and scholarships. Unlike many undergraduate scholarships, those in graduate school are more often awarded on the basis of grades rather than need, so even the well-off students may apply for them. But it is imperative that you maintain outstanding grades, especially today when universities are spending less on student aid than ever, making competition that much stiffer. Individuals often leave large sums of money to schools for scholarships in some field and these can often be quite generous, running into the thousands of dollars per person.

Departments have private access to scholarship funds as well. Within the budget for any given department is a sum alloted for assistantships in order to provide professors with graduate students to help them do their research and teaching. Some departments also have been given money by private companies and individuals to help their students. The Ford Foundation, for example, has been quite active in establishing scholarships. Some departmental grants are only for dissertation research; others are simply no-interest loans or travel funds. As early as possible after your arrival on campus, find out from students and professors about your department's funds; you may have accidentally landed in a department that is both rich and generous. Since they have had more alumni, the older universities have more money for graduate expenses than younger schools. But this varies throughout the country. You will never know if your department is rich or not until you are actually enrolled as a student in its program. But remember: It is still generally easier to obtain financial assistance at the graduate level than at the undergraduate level.

If you are a part-time student working for a government or company, you may find that your employer will pay for your tuition and books. Indeed, today most part-time students have their expenses picked up by their employers.

APPLYING FOR GRANTS

If you are going to apply for university or departmental aid, find out as early in the school year as possible what the deadlines are for submitting application forms, letters or recommendation, and other documentation. The same applies to grants from outside the university. As a rule, you must apply about a year in advance for a grant; therefore, plan for the future and not one month before you need more money. Six months into your graduate program is about the earliest that one can appeal for a for a grant, so start early. Be careful to study the forms and requirements for aid. In preparing applications, you will probably have to write a small essay about yourself and your work. Prepare one that fits their requirements as closely as possible. The procedure should be almost the same as applying for admission to school. Pay attention to deadlines and observe them religiously. Line up your letters early, and make sure that they are sent in on time. Have a professor comment on your essay for style, content, and point of view so that it fits the grant. Pick a half-dozen funds to apply for, beginning with your number one choice and ending with the one you are most certain to win.

In the application procedure, the letters of recommendation and the transcripts always seem to cause problems for students. Before writing a professor's name down on the application form as a character reference, be polite enough to ask that person in advance if he or she would be willing to write the letter. Then check back occasionally to make sure the letter was written and mailed. Try not to impose on one person for too many letters, since these are time-consuming to write. Although you will be asking your college and university to submit your transcripts, which will cost you about one to four dollars each, to the grant institutions, you must follow up to make sure the transcripts were sent. Often they are not sent, and the grant people will sometimes notify you that they have not yet received a letter or grades. One way to determine if your grades have been sent out is not to pay for the transcripts when you order them mailed but instead ask that you be billed for any expenses, pretending you do not know that there are any. Then if you do not receive a bill within a month or so, you can assume that the transcripts were never sent out. Write the school about it: If they were mailed and there was no charge, consider this a rare moment in your academic life, because the school probably will charge for transcripts in the future.

With the letters of recommendation, you simply have to ask the professor if they were sent out. Usually the people you ask are your major professor and two others in whose classes you have done well. On rare occasions, the professor will give you a carbon copy of the letter or a photocopy of the form he or she may have had to fill out on you; but do not count on it, because professors do not like to tell students what they wrote. Usually today, as a rule, you can examine your personal files kept by a university. Such records would include grades and letters of recommendation; thus you could, by asking university officials, see what others have written about you. Such files are becoming increasingly available to students. Wherever this is the case, you must understand that a professor will put into writing only what will not get him into trouble, either because of a possible student lawsuit or because of university regulations regarding comments on students.

There is one other point about graduate aid which needs clarification. Let each of the institutions or universities that offers you money know whether or not you intend to accept their offers. Most scholarships have a stipulation that you cannot use their funds concurrently with another. Consequently, you must often choose the best scholarship that is offered, and usually you must make your choice within a restricted time period. Once you have made your decision, let all the funding sources know that you have either accepted or declined their generosity. If you do not reply one way or the other within a reasonable period, the granting institution will probably assume that you do not wish to accept their funds and will assign them to some other student.

Because the amount of financial aid to graduate students can vary, you need to explore the possibility of winning one or more grants. Assistantships, for which you work a few hours a week, may range from just $400 or $500 up to about $3,000 per school year. The same applies to scholarships, research grants, and dissertation fellowships. Grants of about $2,000 are not uncommon; and with that kind of money, you can pay either tuition and book costs or rent—and probably some other expenses as well. In combination with a working spouse or with help from your family, finances would pose few problems to you.

TAXES

If you have to work for your financial aid, the money you earn is subject to federal income tax. In regard to state income tax, you will have to check with your university. Ordinarily, fellowships and research grants are not subject to federal or state income tax, although they need to be listed as income and accompanied by a statement to the effect that this is fellowship money. Your department or university will provide you with such a declaration upon request, and it must be attached to your income tax forms. For the most current regulations, consult the Internal Revenue Service's tax booklet published each January. You must also check this tax booklet (available at all post offices and at IRS offices) to determine whether or not your parents can still claim you as a dependent if you are receiving financial aid from them and from outside sources as well. The determining factor is often the percentage of expenses borne by your parents for schooling. Because this varies from year to year, every January you must check the new tax regulations.

Those working on dissertations should keep track of all expenses incurred with the project. Save all receipts and canceled checks, because if you ever publish the manuscript as a book you will be able to deduct research and writing expenses from your royalties. All expenses incurred for a five year period back may often be counted and could result in a low tax base for your royalties when spread over several years. When the time comes for you to publish your dissertation, check with the IRS on how to take advantage of this tax rule, since the law is always changing. Ideally, if you can keep a ledger book, make entries as you go along, and put your receipts in a folder or large yellow envelope, this will be acceptable to the IRS. Doing this will also give you an idea of what a fortune you have spent on the project. Unless you publish articles for which you are paid, it is not worth the effort to keep track of non-dissertation expenses.

One method you can use to avoid paying additional income tax in the spring is to claim no dependents for deduction purposes throughout the year. If you receive assistantship pay, on a biweekly or monthly basis, the university's paymaster will deduct income tax. The university will subtract less if you claim dependents and you may even end up owing the government a few dollars as a result. By claiming zero dependents, the chances are that the government will owe you money, since too much will have been deducted from your pay check. And there is nothing like receiving a green check from Uncle Sam in the spring. If you are married, both of you should declare no dependents until you file your joint income tax form. The refund can be large by student standards and might possibly cover a summer's tuition. If you need help on not claiming dependents, check with the head secretary in your department, since this person is probably in charge of making sure that you fill out a tax witholding form for the university. The local IRS people will also answer your questions regarding student taxes. If there is more than one IRS office in town, ask the same questions of several officials, because their answers may vary at times and you may have to obtain a consensus opinion.

ASSISTANTSHIPS

There are essentially two forms of work a graduate student can do that are connected with the department and for which one will be paid by the university: helping a professor or teaching undergraduates. Since most of the financial aid a student receives is available in the form of an assistantship, having one can play an important part in your academic life. Bound closely would also be your role as a teacher. You would develop certain types of research skills, be associated with a particular professor's own work, and gain experience lecturing and evaluating students.

An assistantship is simply a job within your department entailing work for one or more professors. Usually you are notified in the spring that you have an assistantship for the fall. They tend to run from September to June, although some continue for twelve months. The number of hours one has to work varies from as little as two hours a week up to twenty hours weekly; but more than that is rare, since most universities require their assistantship people to be full-time students. Your salary will, in most cases, be calculated on an hourly basis: The more you work, the higher the pay. The number of hours you actually work per week is also established at the time you are informed of the assistantship. Students, as a rule, would rather have an assistantship than a part-time job somewhere else on campus or in town, because the work may often be in their field of interest. Very few universities allow their graduates to work at another job while holding an assistantship. The chances of getting caught may be slight; but if you are found out, your department may never recommend that you receive university aid in the future. Their argument is that the money given to you allows you to spend most of your time working on your studies.

The kind of work done can cover a wide range of duties. Some students will occasionally lecture to freshmen for a professor who is out of town at a convention or is detained by other business. Others grade papers, check class rolls, set up and tear down lab experiments, do clerical work, conduct research, and run errands. Since most people holding assistantships only work for one professor, the kind of work they do may vary. But the duties can be enjoyable if, for example, they are in your area of specialization and if the professor you work with exerts an effort to make the work challenging yet not time-consuming. Some professors use their assistants to do their dull academic chores, while others treat this as another means of teaching their people more skills.

Since you are required to work a certain number of hours weekly, you will have to keep in touch with your professor at least once a week for assignments. If you do not work the maximum hours that you are supposed to, you are not docked any pay unless you are really derelict in your responsibilities. For example, if you have to work ten hours and you put in only five or less because of a lack of assignments, you would not be risking your appointment. One thing students often do is avoid working, and this is understood by many professors, since their assistants have a great deal to study. Some professors welcome not having to dream up work for their assistants, while others will slave them to death. One of the tricks often used is to avoid being in the department when your boss has office hours or comes in for mail. And for the stickler who wants every minute of work he or she can get out of you, just render unto Caesar what he is entitled to and no more. Do not try to satisfy such an individual—you never will, and it could cost you your grades if you fall behind in your studies. If a professor demands more work out of you than he or she is supposed to—and this happens quite often—first try to make yourself scarce in order to avoid any clashes. If this fails, go to see your department chairman, who will usually understand that your studies come first. He or she will probably take care of the situation. If your boss persists, have the chairman assign you to some other professor. If the slave driver happens to be the chairman, you are out of luck.

One problem many students feel about their assistantship work is that their assignments are not helpful to their education or career because they are made to do clerical work or run errands. But remember that this is a job for which you are being paid; if you worked in a hamburger joint in town, the work would be farther away from your field than that you might be doing in the department. This point should also be kept in mind by those students who do research for professors which result in publications for which the student receive no credit. You are paid for that work, and you are also gaining experience doing publishable research. Researching without named credit is a practice not solely limited to universities. This is common in industry and government as well, where even whole books will be written by one person whose name does not appear on the cover, yet who has been paid for his or her services.

No student will be assigned work not related to departmental business. If someone asks you to clean house, cook, wax a car, or do anything which is not university business, go see your chairman, and, if need be, one of the deans. The university is not paying you to be somebody's private servant! As a graduate assistant, you may be asked—not told—to help out on some project in which the department is involved; and even though you would not have to participate, you should consider doing so. This might include helping out at registration at your department's table, assisting at their picnics and parties, or playing on the department's softball team. At these affairs, people are always needed to move stuff, to set things up, or to do some running around, and usually the graduate students are chosen for these tasks. As an assistant, you are really a minor appendage of the department's "establishment," and this entails certain minor social obligations. In some departments, the students themselves will want to run the mixed professor-student parties, ball games, and other social functions, and these may also involve students who do not have assistantships.

As in every facet of your graduate career, be diplomatic when you run up against problems. Think before you object about your work, especially to your boss. If you are thinking about complaining to the chairman, make sure that your boss is not on your committee. Do your work without arguments and always give the impression that you are eager for new assignments. Remember that you are being judged by your work as much as by your classroom performance. If you do well, everyone will know about it; and this is important when it comes time to write letters of recommendation to potential employers.

For those who are independent minded and who do not work well in a team, try to find a professor to work for—if you are permitted this latitude in choice (many places do permit this)—who will give you maximum freedom of action in determining the nature and level of your productivity. Also, push for an assignment with an important professor, because he may well be willing to write you a letter of recommendation. Research assistantships will often lead you to potential dissertation topics. If you do not already have one in mind, work for someone who will make you do research. Doing this kind of labor for a superstar can enhance your future professional reputation, since you will be able to say "I worked with Professor _____."

THE STUDENT PROFESSOR

If you are one of the brighter students in the department with excellent grades and an M.A., you may be given a choice between having a regular assistantship or teaching a course. Usually, teaching one or possibly two classes means a small increase in pay. More important, you get to teach freshman and sophomores, the very people you will probably first instruct when you leave graduate school (assuming that you want to be a professor). This is a chance to clock in some practical experience. If given a choice, think three times before tossing aside this opportunity. If you plan to be a professor, accept the teaching responsibility, even though you will be paid less for your work than a professor teaching the same class. When you leave school, that experience may mean the difference between finding a job and not finding a job. It also gives you an excuse to prepare a set of lecture notes, something which you will not have much time for after you leave school. Often the student teacher (TA) will instruct the introductory college course in his field. Freshman math, western civilization, English literature survey, elementary chemistry, and physical education are the sorts of courses often taught by TAs. Very rarely, a student with some unique specialization may even have an opportunity to teach a more advanced course for undergraduates.

Besides monetary considerations, teaching carries with it certain advantages. You may be assigned an office of your own or be allowed to share one with a fellow TA. You then have space in which to do your own studying; this is especially valuable if you hate the library and if your residence is too crowded or too noisy. Often, you will be allowed to use departmental stationery. Armed with your class responsibilities and departmental stationery, you can order free copies of the various textbooks used in the course you teach. Some people abuse this by ordering everything in sight, which is a real rip-off of the publishing industry, but more on that later. For once, anyway, you are at the firing end of education, looking down the barrel of the classroom instead of up into it. In short, you find out how the teacher feels at the front of the room. Prestige in the department goes with teaching, as well as a sense that now you are working yourself out of the role of student. And it is an ego trip for many people.

Many departments have a policy of having as many of their students as possible teach in order to round out their preparation for academic careers. Most graduate programs in education, for example, make teaching mandatory. Departments will also count the hours you teach as credit for the total number of hours you must take per quarter or semester in order to retain full-time status. In such cases, grades are rarely assigned, except for the S or U; and you will never hear of someone receiving a U for teaching. Departments assign one or more faculty members to help TAs. They give advice; answer questions; drop into class periodically to check on a TA's performance; help prepare exams; and suggest policies regarding absences, grades, and tests. Although the amount of guidance varies; there is usually some. Since the professors assigned to this task are often experienced teachers and outstanding lecturers, you can really learn a great deal from them. Teaching is not as easy as it looks, and you will need all the help you can find.

Although there is no room in this book to describe how to teach, some suggestions can be made. Collect copies of tests and exams given by other people who teach the same course you do in order to have a large reservoir of questions to draw from. Because making up good questions is very difficult and time-consuming, this can help. You might have a professor comment on your test questions before they are mimeographed. Ask others what they do in regard to testing, assigning papers, and lecturing. You might even look over other teachers' lecture notes to see the nature of the material being covered. Remember: It has been years since you took the course you are about to teach, and probably your recollection of what went on then is rapidly fading.

Check with the other professors to see if there are any departmental rules governing absences, the number of tests required, cheating, plagiarism, make-ups, changing and recording grades, exam policies, hours of lab that must be given, or special guidelines regarding the use of lectures and class participation activities. Often there are few or no overall rules governing class policy, but investigate anyway: You do not want situations developing where you are found irresponsible. Protect yourself at all stages of teaching from faculty, student, and parental criticisms by keeping some sort of roll; by announcing your grading policies at the start of the course; by giving tests which can be graded with numerical marks; and then by keeping all papers, tests, and roll sheets for at least three months after the course is completed. This way, if any question about a grade comes up, you have all the documents involved.

Plan on spending as much time preparing a course as you would in taking it. The educational handbooks are right: It really does take several hours of work for every hour you teach, assuming that you do the job properly. If you know long in advance when and what you will be teaching, you might begin to plan what will be covered in each hour of class and actually start writing lecture notes. There is nothing pleasant about having to prepare for tomorrow's class; and since you are the teacher, you must *always* be ready with something to talk about. There is no excuse for being unorganized. Today, most universities allow their students to pass judgment on their instructor's performance, usually at the end of a course, by filling out the computer answer sheet of a questionaire. If you did a poor job, your students will say so; and the chairman of your department will see the results of the questionnaire. That will not look good when it comes time for a job. And if you really are irresponsible, you may not be teaching in your university much longer.

Sometimes you can pick what segment of a full year course you would like to teach, provided that you volunteer to teach at some unpopular hour. Requesting a class and hour has to be done at least one quarter or semester in advance, when future classes and times are still being blocked out. An excellent time to teach is at eight o'clock in the morning. Few professors like working at that hour, so you should be able to select virtually any class taught then. Teaching at eight is not that bad; it is certainly easier than taking a course at that hour. You are forced to get up an hour or more before you lecture in order to be wide awake and to have time to review your materials. If you take a course at that hour, you probably would not get up until half-past seven or fifteen minutes before class, so you stumble in feeling miserable and half asleep. As an instructor, you could not do this. By teaching early in the morning, you will also be pushing your obligation out of the way, thereby avoiding conflicts with classes you want to take, since few graduate courses are taught at eight o'clock. You then have the whole day to devote to your studies. As a rule, eight o'clock classes are also smaller, and that means less papers to grade. On top of all this, by volunteering to teach at that horrible hour you look like a hero in the department, willingly taking on a nasty task.

If you try teaching at ten in the morning, there is almost bound to be a class conflict with a course you want; or you are more likely to have a large class of students and be stuck with a particular segment of the course you wanted to avoid. In the natural sciences, you are probably going to be assigned to run a lab, usually in the afternoon, and there is little you can do about that. For those of you who are not in the natural sciences, avoid teaching in the afternoons or at night, since this is prime study and research time. Mornings should be given up for attending and teaching classes, having your office hours, and taking care of any paper work that may face you. This formula works fairly well for most students and should for you. If you have nothing to do in the morning you will undoubtedly sleep until ten or eleven o'clock thereby losing valuable work time. Teaching in the morning will at least force you out of bed.

The expansion of student bodies at the undergraduate and graduate levels has resulted in the extended use of TAs. In many large universities, freshmen rarely have a full professor or even an associate professor as a teacher. More likely than not, a graduate student will be their instructor. Coupled with this expanded reliance upon graduate students has been a heated controversy about their use. Universities argue that they need this cheap labor in order to handle the ever growing number of freshmen. Their use allows the faculty to concentrate on research and on teaching juniors, seniors and graduate students. Departments contend that by using graduates they can offer more courses for upper classmen. Furthermore, it is cheaper for a university to have a TA teaching a class than a professor.

Some students, both freshman and graduate, argue that this is low grade slave labor and a growing number of educators and parents agree, maintaining that the quality of instruction for freshmen declines when TAs teach. They also feel that universities have little interest in what is taught to their freshmen. Some students contend that the system of using students as assistants and instructors permits a university to keep a person enrolled longer than might otherwise be necessary. Universities are accused of trying to increase the number of students a department can claim by using TAs. The more students a department can claim, the more professors it can hire and the bigger its budget will be. This argument is especially used with state legislatures which are impressed by numbers of students in relation to faculty and dollars. Also, a professor does not want to risk being dismissed during an austerity drive because he or she has too few students. Such an individual may try to hold on to those he or she has for as long as possible by making sure they receive financial aid. Teaching ensures that some students will be on campus beyond the point when they might have left because of monetary considerations. And by making teaching experience almost a prerequisite for a teaching job in today's tight market, a student is virtually compelled to submit to this system.

However, one of the biggest problems facing a TA is the conflict that arises between the dual roles of student and teacher. Given a certain amount of time and work to do in studying and in teaching, should one sacrifice teaching responsibilities to get studies done or does teaching come first? This is a dilemma challenging most TAs. For some, the question is a minor one because they are able to juggle the two roles with little difficulty, while others find it a real headache. There are students who will sacrifice teaching responsibilities in order to study or to do dissertation research, feeling that their work is more important than taking care of their students. Some reverse it and consequently take forever to finish their dissertations. This conflict has been recognized as a serious one by educators and has been the subject of much controversy, but is still remains with us.

The problem of the TA's dual role is something that you will have to solve in your own way. You do have a responsibility to your students, but you also have one to yourself. How you handle the two will depend a great deal on your level of productivity, on the work you have to do, and on the facility with which you can meet the demands of both teaching and studying. If you feel that the department is keeping you longer than is necessary for you to finish the degree work, then you might make the decision to stop teaching. Although this will mean a loss of income, it will not necessarily hurt your job chances, since you will by then have had some public speaking experience. It really makes little difference whether you have had one, two, or three years of teaching behind you, just as long as you have some experience.

3
Graduate Course Work

A STUDENT'S
PROGRAM COMMITTEE

Since a graduate student's fate is really determined more by the whims of his or her committee than just by his or her performance, picking a major professor may be the most important discision you will make in school. To a lesser extent, choosing the rest of a committee is also of vital importance and must be done with great care. Because all students have to select major professors and other faculty for their committees early, it is imperative that this be executed after careful consideration of what one wishes to major and minor in, followed by an estimation of whether there will be any clashes with potential committee members.

Your major professor is the most important teacher you will have. As your boss, he or she rules with absolute power. In effect, this professor tells you what courses to take, helps you as your expertise in his or her field develops, and directs your thesis and probably your dissertation as well. Such a person is the moving force behind any university aid that comes your way; and when you have finished your graduate education, he or she will help you find a job, especially if you are seeking a job in the college teaching profession. Often, whether or not you make it through graduate school will depend on who you pick for a major professor. However, such a decision can be made with some confidence, even early in your graduate career.

The first thing students will tell you is to pick a senior faculty member with broad experience in dealing with graduate students.

Select someone who has directed numerous theses and dissertations. Young professors are inexperienced and tend to overwork their students out of some fear that they themselves are not up to par, either in order to establish their level in the department's pecking order or out of ignorance. Such ego lifting exercises are rarely practiced by senior personnel who already know not to expect too much from graduate students and who are more aware of what a student's limitations are. Having taught for a long time, they have made their mistakes on others before you came along. A senior professor has influence within the university, and this can be of great importance when it comes to finding money for students. It is well known that, as a generalization, senior people find more grants and aid for their students than do young professors. Older teachers are better known in the profession as well; and consequently, when your work is done, often who you studied under can be as important as what you studied.

A second rule you might go by is to take a course with the person under whom you are thinking of majoring in order to see if the two of you get along with each other. You must try to know the professor's standards before the selection is made. Of course, before taking courses under any professor, ask the other students what he or she is like as a teacher, as a dissertation director, and as an individual. Also ask whether the professor is unreasonable in his or her standards and grading. No use picking someone who has a two by four chip on his or her shoulder.

Select a professor with whom you have no personality clashes, an instructor you like and who you think will return the feeling. Mutual respect is of prime importance, since you will be seeing a great deal of each other. He or she will be guiding your intellectual development, giving you suggestions regarding your life as a graduate student, and offering the kind of advice this book suggests. Therefore, pick someone who knows the inner workings of the department, the graduate school, and the profession. In order to do this, you often have to choose a fairly competent, even a highly demanding individual. It is better that you be exposed to some hard work and high standards than that you encounter these for the first time when you leave graduate school.

But it is very important to pick the top person in the department whose field of interest coincides with yours. If you find that the department's superstar is an expert in Egyptian archaeology and you cannot stand Egypt, do not select this individual, as there are bound to be other competent people in the department to work under. In choosing a field, you should first ask professors and students if the area is already jammed with graduate trained people; if it is, you should select a less crowded field. This is simply a matter you will have to gamble on, since there is no guarantee that when you finish school your choice will have been a wise one.

The principles behind picking the rest of your committee are the same as those you use in selecting a major professor, whether it is for the M.A. or the Ph.D. Regarding the latter, it is important that your decisions be made after extra deliberation, since you will be working with these people for an even longer period of time. It would be foolish to select a professor who plans to retire soon or one who is in poor health, because in either instance, completion of your graduate education could be delayed. Have your faculty friends on your committee, even if it means minoring in some area that does not thrill you; at least you will have less to worry about as a result. If a professor dislikes you, under no circumstances do you put such a person on your committee. Avoid even taking a course from him or her. You cannot afford to risk a C or even a B. The one exception to the general rules above would be to put a young professor who is also a friend on your committee. As a rule, older instructors are safer, but if a younger person appears sympathetic to you, consider asking this individual to join your committee. This is a case where you have to play it by ear, guessing at what the situation is like in your department.

Once you have formed your committee, it is difficult—if not impossible—to ask someone to step down. Consider yourself stuck with a permanent marriage. The only time changes can be made without causing embarrassment or hard feelings is at the end of your Ph.D. comps. At this point, if you want to juggle your committee around in order to put people on it who would be more helpful to you on the dissertation, this is understood. You can go to others and invite them to join, but do so with the prior permission of your major professor. Some students will drop professors either because of developing personality clashes with them or because one professor, who may be a good teacher, never writes or directs dissertations and knows nothing about your topic. When you drop a professor from a committee, do it with tact. Argue, for example, that the dissertation is in an entirely different field from that of the professor.

Whatever the reasons may be, pick your new people with caution. Choose professors who have published extensively and who have directed dissertations. They can help you to tighten up your logic and writing style to a considerable extent. Also, choose people who have some knowledge of your topic—or as close to some idea about it as possible—in order that they may be able to suggest novel interpretations, new sorces of information, and a fresh manner of presentation. The right senior people who serve on your committee may also be able to use their contacts to help you to find a publisher for your dissertation. They will use their influence for someone they have worked with before helping an unknown student.

By asking a professor to join your dissertation committee, you are in a sense flattering the individual, since you are expressing respect and confidence in his or her abilities. A professor's status is partly measured by the number of students working under him or her: the more students, the greater the image. You might remember, however, that if a professor has too many students, he or she will not be able to give you the kind of individual attention that you deserve. There are professors who never say no who will serve on anybody's committee. If you discover that a particular professor is directing ten dissertations and a dozen theses and is sitting on twenty committees, forget him. Good luck in ever seeing such a person, let alone having your work read with care!

At the master's level, committees are formed in much the same way as at the dissertation stage and usually have no more than three members. Doctoral committees are never less than four and rarely over seven. In both cases, the major professor will suggest members, and the student, in most instances, has the final word on who is included. If you do not get along with someone that your professor wants, say so; chances are that he or she will understand and that the objectionable name will be forgotten.

When you are finally defending your dissertation (more of a ritual than an exam), anyone can sit in on the hour or two hour oral. As a matter of fact, the date of your final performance is often published in the faculty newsletter, and some people—such as old personality clashes—may turn up that you wish would not.

Have little fear: You have passed before the exam started, otherwise your committee would never have allowed you to type and duplicate the final draft of your dissertation for the university's files. If someone who is not on your committee decides to give you a hard time, do not worry: He does not sign the approval sheet. Such vindictive behavior is very rare and in many departments it is unheard of. It has to be mentioned, however, since nasty professors can be found on every campus.

CARE AND FEEDING OF THE MAJOR PROFESSOR

Since success or failure in graduate school depends a great deal of the relationship you have with your major professor, you must make this person happy with your performance even if it does injury to your pride or to your views. There is no faster way to self-destruct than having open warfare with the all-powerful major professor. Essentially, your success will depend on your academic performance but also on your abilities as a politician-diplomat. This combined role as student and politico should not be a difficult one to play if you have picked your mentor wisely. If he or she is competent, you will be molded into a scholar as your skills and knowledge develop. You will be defended from other faculty members who may find faults with your work, and, as a rule, your financial aid will improve. Finally, the experience, contacts, and prestige of this individual often make the difference between just a job and a desirable position, especially if you want to teach. Therefore, it behooves you to treat your mentor with respect and obedience.

Students have found that certain fundamental principles govern this relationship, principles that vary only according to the personalities of the professor and the neophyte scholar. You must begin to know each other; and what better way is there than to take most or all of the professor's courses? In these classes, later on while writing your thesis or dissertation, and in general conversation with your mentor, avoid acrimonious arguments and do not express opinions which you know will throw him or her into a rage. Never embarrass the professor if, for example, he or she should be incorrect in making some statement in class or in front of others. Bad blood could lead to low grades and hard times in school. How far you should go along with these guidelines

57

*Graduate
Course
Work*

depends on the individuals involved. You simply have to judge for yourself how to live with your mentor. Some students are very close to their professors, while others have a highly formalized relationship. Some mentors are humble, quiet individuals, while others are bombastic, loud primadonnas. Most students like their professors, while others hate them. Since no two cases are really alike, you are very much on your own.

Occasionally, your mentor will invite you to his or her home to dinner or to a party for students or faculty; or he or she may take you some place in order to introduce you to friends or useful colleagues. In these social situations, develop a friendship with the people to whom you are introduced. If you have good relations with the family, this can lead to a lot of free meals over a several year period. If the two of you get along in graduate school, the odds are that your friendship will be a close one over the years. This friendship evolves from a student-teacher relationship to one between two colleagues and is one of the most fundamental relationships you will ever develop in the academic world, so nurture it well. In order to develop a closer working association outside of class and home, do your assistantship work under the major professor if it is at all possible. Chances are that he or she will put you to work on some project of mutual interest, while another professor may not. Working under your mentor will give each of you an opportunity to develop admiration for the other which is a key ingredient to success.

There are certain rules of etiquette which should also govern your relations with the major professor. Always keep him or her informed about what courses you are taking, since this individual will probably have to sign a registration form giving approval anyway. Discuss any master plan you may have concerning how and when you intend to take classes, study for comps, and do research. You will find that he or she may be able to improve your thinking simply because of having had experience in these matters. Treat your professor with the utmost respect. Although you may, upon invitation, call certain young professors by their first names, never, never call your mentor by his or hers. And because he or she is supposedly a friend as well as a teacher, you should defend him against the criticisms of others, just as he or she will, in most cases, protect you. Present your mentor with a hardbound copy of your thesis or dissertation. If you publish any articles or books either in graduate school or afterwards, give your professor autographed copies, especially if the article or book happens to be related to your dissertation.

As an aspiring young scholar, you should get into the habit of discussing your field with your mentor outside of class. The extent of your talks will be subject to such conditions as his or her office hours and the encouragement he or she gives you. These exercises can be mutually profitable, since both of you can cover material that can not be discussed in class in a pleasant way. As a rule, it is not presumptuous for you to ask for copies of his or her publications; but ask only after you have been a student for many months. Read them and possibly discuss their contents with the author. Most students want their professor's publications as souvenirs of graduate school, and hard-to-come-by publications can usually be found in duplicate on your mentor's book shelf. Periodically, your professor will invite you to some professional conference or to some social or academic function, often to show you off as a prize student. Think twice before saying that you cannot attend. These are academic activities that you really should participate in, and they can be enjoyable. In many ways, the professor is acting like a proud parent on such occasions. The message you must understand is that your contacts with the professor are not solely bound by the classroom but that they encompass a variety of situations and conditions.

There are several summary commandments you might keep in mind regarding major professors. Do not pick just anyone in haste, as many students do during the first term in school. Be as selective as if you were finding a spouse. If you act rashly, you may live to regret the decision. Yet again, do not put off picking someone for too long. If you take six months, that is reasonable; if you take one year, that may be too slow. Remember that you need a mentor as soon after you arrive on campus as is possible.

Under no circumstances should you select a professor who is either on the verge of retiring or in bad health. The reason for this is quite simple. Should he or she die part way through your program, you would have to select a new mentor who may not like the way your education has progressed and who could delay your graduation until you have satisfied his requirements. This is especially possible at the thesis or dissertation stage. You might be half-way through the writing when your new professor may ask you to start all over again, tackling your project differently;

this could cost you an extra year or more of work. This problem must be kept in mind because it is not so uncommon: It happens all the time. Also, a dead mentor would be of no use to you in finding you financial aid, getting you a job, or introducing you to prominent members of your profession. This point may sound cold-blooded, but it is something students often overlook which can have disastrous consequences.

CLASSES

Graduate classes are organized in much the same way as undergraduate courses. The intellectual level of the work is really not that much higher, either. What you have that is different is more work. If an undergraduate has to read three books in a course, the graduate student has to read a possible seven; the undergraduate assignment of three book reviews turns into five for graduate students; the "no term paper" notice in an undergraduate course converts into a major research project for graduate students. Essentially, you will pass through classes much as you did when you were an undergraduate; consequently, there is no need to discuss them here. What needs commenting on is the problem of regular and overload schedules.

Full loads are taken mostly for the same reasons as at the undergraduate level: to complete a program in a normal period of time, because your family will wonder why you are taking forever to finish your degree, or because you are forced to finish by the terms of a scholarship or an employer. In graduate school, the reasons for taking a full load can be more complicated, especially since a normal number of courses is a great deal of work. For many students, it is too much, causing them to opt for something less than the minimum full program. Many students need to be full-time in order to hold onto an assistantship or fellowship, to use university housing, (which may be cheaper in terms of cost per hour), to conform to ROTC regulations, or because the G.I. Bill requires it. Also, some students just want to get out of graduate school quickly.

Then there are those who will take overloads, which means that they register for more than three or four courses per quarter or semester. Students will sometimes do this in order to hurry through a program or to place a certain number of thesis or dissertation hours on their record, especially if they are doing this kind of work while taking classes. Or, they take a language while registered for a normal load in their field. But taking an overload, if it does not consist just of courses in your field, may in fact be less work than carrying a normal number of classes. For this reason, you will find friends who have signed up for seventeen or even twenty hours at a time.

What one does is to match a time-consuming course with one requiring little work, applying much the same technique that undergraduates do. Just to chock up hours, you might sign up for a noncredit language course which you do not have to attend. People often use this technique as a means of having status as a full-time student carrying a required number of hours while taking only one course less for grade. For example, if, in your school, a full load consists of three courses but you only want to take two because they are time-demanding, then you could register for a language reading knowledge class as number three and just never go to it. You do not get grades for that noncredit course anyway. Some universities will charge you for these "phantom hours," but others do not. It is possible to find students who take only two courses and who fill the rest of the time with thesis or dissertation hours up to and beyond the minimum hours needed to be listed as a full-time student; yet these students often work less than the person who is carrying only twelve or fifteen hours.

Another popular trick is to sign up for a larger course load, or for seminars, colloquies and directed individual study hours (DIS) in substitution for courses. Usually, these can take less time than courses since there are few or no classes to attend. You only read books or write a paper for each, all of which requires fewer hours than sitting in a lecture hall and doing the outside assignments. For those unfamiliar with the DIS, these are credit hours which you can sign up for (with the department's approval) in order to read on some subject of concern to you or to write a paper on a topic for which there is no related course. In some universities, the DIS can be a substitute for seminars and are so used if no seminars which interest the student are offered.

While going through graduate school, you may find that you are running out of courses to take. Or, for one reason or another, you may find that it would be to your advantage to take an overload or to juggle the normal load to fit unusual conditions. Whatever the case, the suggestions made above are only a few of the more common means employed to solve workload problems. Others will suggest themselves because of your particular university and special departmental rules. No doubt, your fellow students will think up ways to avoid work or to solve any serious class problems inherent in your program. When in doubt, consult your peers and your major professor for ideas. You may also be lucky to have a professor in your department blessed with a knack for solving problems of this sort who is willing to help you. Remember: There are as many ways of doing graduate work as there are students, and the combination of classes you take can be unique.

WRITTEN AND ORAL EXAMS

Testing procedures in graduate school differ from those in your undergraduate days because they serve different purposes. Preparation for and writing of exams do deserve much care, since in many classes your final is the only test score in the course. If there is no term paper or collection of lab reports to turn in, it may be your only grade.

Your professors will often assume that you know more than undergraduates and that you can write a good essay. They expect quality performance, so try not to disappoint them. Invariably, you will take your tests in blue books. In a rare case, a professor will allow a student to type essay answers or to compose them on a typewriter, particularly if his handwriting is abominable or if the student can convince the professor that his or her writing style improves on the machine. Take-home exams are also popular and lend themselves to interpretative essays. In such a case, your product should be the result of some thought and several drafts. All typed material should be double-spaced on eight by eleven sheets.

Written exams are given at the end of almost all lecture courses and even in some colloquies or seminars. They are sometimes used in preliminary Ph.D. exams taken after the M.A. to determine if a student should continue with his studies, although these exams tend to be oral. Written tests are usually used in M.A. and Ph.D. comps in combination with orals. The written doctoral exams may take a week or more to write at a pace of four to six hours per day. They may be the take-home variety or they may be conducted in class. Invariably, the written comps are essay rather than objective exams. Check with your friends to find out what the local story is on how to write them.

Oral examinations are quite popular in graduate school. Usually, you will run into them at the M.A. comps and at the thesis defense, in doctoral preliminary exams, in your Ph.D. comps, with your dissertation prospectus, and finally, in your dissertation defense. Generally speaking, the defense of your thesis or dissertation lasts about one hour; sometimes it is longer. If things are going well, the defense may take an even shorter time. In these defenses, the student can dominate the conversation and can actually guide the direction in which the discussion flows. The more difficult oral exam is that given to test a field of knowledge.

Oral field exams are very tricky. More often than not, they are given after the writtens for the M.A. and Ph.D. comps. Your written essays are supposed to point out your weaknesses, and from these, your professors have an idea of the type of questions to ask you. The questioning may be logical and may cover material in some sort of order, or it may be haphazard or very trivial and detailed. On the other hand, questions can be basic ones which pose no problem to you. The pattern depends entirely on the professors involved. Their usual behavior on exams is often well known to the other students. Find out what they know and use their experiences as a determining factor in picking a committee and then in preparing for the orals.

How much time each member of your committee has with you in comps varies with each school, but rarely is it over one hour apiece. Yet numerous questions can be asked, even in twenty minutes. The problem you have is to field each question as it comes and to eat up the time without letting too many unanswerable questions slip by. When you find a question you know nothing about, say so and hope that the professor will move on to other things. But avoid having to admit ignorance too often. When you get a question you are familiar with, expound on the subject until someone tells you to stop. If you can, guide the discussion by raising related points upon which you are prepared to comment at length. Another way to pass time is to prod an especially talkative professor into answering either his own question or someone else's. An ideal situation is to promote an argument between two committee members, while you just watch and occasionally nod your head in approval. If you are doing poorly, your major professor may jump in and interrupt in order to direct the questions onto ground he or she knows you can handle. Work out in advance with your mentor the approximate order of the professors, questions, ending with a field in which you feel competent. When they vote on passing or failing you, hopefully they will have forgotten your blank spaces and will remember the last few minutes of questioning.

Often individual committee members have made up their minds about whether to pass or fail you before the orals come up. They may even make this decision before your writtens are given. Unless you really do poorly or brilliantly, prior views on your qualifications will probably not be altered. In a sense, your fate is not in your hands when the exams come up. Your job will be to make sure confidence in you is not shaken during the exam period—a considerable undertaking in its own right. In general, your committee is not out to flunk you, but they will try to make sure that you are competent. Giving oral exams provides them with the flexible opportunity they need during which to test your knowledge.

A word should be said about preliminary oral exams. These tests last from one to three hours. Since the prelims have as their purpose determining if you know at least the rudiments of a subject, your performance can be less than brilliant. These tests are used as a check on students who have transferred into your department with an M.A. from some other school in order to make sure that they have really learned something before. They are used as a means of weeding out students the department feels should not be allowed to continue on toward the Ph.D., and they are also used as a periodic check to confirm the progress of one's own people. Preparation for these tests is recommended by most professors, who usually suggest more study than is actually necessary. Often, the only thing you may have to do is to read several good textbooks in order to familiarize yourself with the basic knowledge on topics that might be the subject of questioning. Check with some of the students to see how they tackled this problem and to find out what kinds of questions they were asked by the professors who are on your committee.

If you are a transfer student, these exams are very important. For those who are continuing on for a Ph.D. in the same department where they earned their M.A., their professors already have some idea about their competency, but this is not so with the new students. If you are one of the latter, it is especially important to do well, since this will be your debut performance. How you answer your examiners may determine, for a while at least, what your reputation will be. You can actually make a good name for yourself in the test, and thereby you can enter your classes without professors entertaining any doubts about your abilities. Even though you never would have been accepted if your grades and recommendations had not been good, professors still mistrust other departments and feel that they may be less demanding of students than your new department. Whether this is the case or not is unimportant: The misgivings about other departments are widespread. Consequently, you have to prove yourself all over again. If you can convince the department, delay taking the prelims for several months in order to give yourself time to find out who will test you. This way, you can help to ensure that your performance will be acceptable.

GRADES

A discussion on grades is included in the section entitled *Differences Between Undergraduate and Graduate Programs* in Chapter 1. It should be noted, however, that the role of grades in graduate school is far different from their role in undergraduate days. They are less important than before as long as they remain good. Everyone has good grades in graduate school: A's are very easy to obtain. Rarely does one see a student with poor marks. Grades become important in that you usually need a 3.5 overall grade point average in graduate school in order to join your field's honorary society as a student member. They are important if you are competing for grants since they go to people with the highest marks. But grades are not that vital for finding jobs, unless again there are a lot of Bs and Cs on your record. Grades diminish in importance if you are trying to publish as well. Students and professors worry less about grades in graduate school than do undergraduates. The factor one worries about is comps, not grades. You can have an A average and flunk the comps, thereby never completing your program: It does happen. There is no security until all the comps have been passed. That is why grades decline in significance. Of course, bad marks will make professors think, and probably with justification, that you are incompetent, stupid, or lazy; and they may reflect this feeling in their letters of recommendation. Strive for high grades, but remember that they are of secondary importance.

Good marks are probably more important to your family than they are to you. Grades are dutifully sent home by the university Registrar as though you were a college freshman. Sometimes your spouse receives them. Often you are the last person to find out officially what your grades are, although professors post their marks on office doors or on classroom walls. Try not to make a big commotion about grades with your professors, since they hardly give any attention to them. For many teachers, giving graduates any grades at all is another piece of time-consuming red tape the university forces upon them. Once in a rare while, there will be a professor who decides to hand out Ds and Fs to graduate students. You probably will not be on campus two days before hearing about such an individual. There are cases where such grades have been given. The normal reaction to this would be to spread the professor's reputation as an unreasonable person and to request that the chairman insert a letter in the student's file affirming the same view. However, on occasion, a poor student really does deserve a D—and gets it. Professors try to avoid issuing Ds and Fs to graduate students because most people immediately assume that it was not the student's fault.

Once you leave graduate school, your grades will depreciate in value. If you go into the teaching profession, the important facts in your background are where you studied and under whom. Even in teaching, after a while your graduate school will fade into insignificance as people ask what your publications are and where have you taught. If you go to work for industry or government, after you have been hired, probably no one will want to see your grades again and possibly they won't even care where you went to school. From that point on, you will be judged according to your job performance and not on the various degrees hanging on your office wall.

NOTES AND FILE SYSTEMS

Everything you learn in graduate school must be remembered, since you are held responsible for all of this material on your M.A. and Ph.D. comps. In addition, doctoral students are also expected to know bibliographical information. Most universities test fields rather than courses taken; but, in some master's programs, exams are based just on courses. Find out as early as possible which way your department tests so that you can plan accordingly. But for either testing system, vast amounts of material have to be learned, hence a highly organized set of notes and files will make preparation for these tests much easier.

By now you should know how to take thorough notes. Keep a complete set for every course you take, because the chances are good that your committee members will ask questions from their courses which you have taken. Since you may be examined on material studied two or more years ago, it would be a good idea to type your notes in outline form as soon as possible after each class, filling in details and checking with other students to confirm that your set is complete. By spending twenty minutes or more after each class typing notes, you have an opportunity to organize the material in a way which will be easy for you to understand years later. You can use this opportunity to correct misspelled names and to write out hastily devised abbreviations.

Make sure that you write down the titles of all the books mentioned by your professors in class, since these may come up later in your exams. Most students find that typing notes double-spaced on 8 x 11 sheets is most convenient since they can be put into a looseleaf ring notebook or letter file cabinet. Also, keep a folder for each course in which to stuff bibliographies, old exams, copies of papers, and all handouts. This material may be of further use to you as a teacher as well as for exam preparation. You might note on the bibliography sheets or in your notes any remarks made in class about the books so that later you can comment on a volume briefly without having to read it.

If time or other circumstances do not permit you to take a course in one of your fields, then find a good set of notes from some other student and copy all of them. This way, you will know what a particular professor thinks about the various points raised in a course, something you would miss by just reading textbooks. Graduate students do share notes and you should learn to do so. If you have pack rat tendencies, graduate school will reinforce them. You may find, as do many other students, that one set of notes for a specific course is not enough and that making a copy of someone else's notes augments your material in a useful way. When professors hand out bibliographies and fact sheets in areas related to your own, ask them for copies. In most cases, they will have extras from their classes which they will be delighted to spread around. Collect these for your appropriate files.

Make notes on all your readings, even if they are only one or two line comments. Ideally, if you start graduate school on the first day by keeping a 3 x 5 or 5 x 8 card bibliography, this will be of immense help for exams and later, if you are a professor, in preparing your own bibliography sheets. Maintain in this file, in alphabetical and topical order, a card on every book you read and one on those commented on by others and which are listed in class handouts. It takes little time to preserve such files from the beginning, while it is time-consuming if you decide six months before your exams to prepare one. If you know a student who has such a collection, either in your field or in a related one, you might copy some of his or her cards in order to round out your collection. In exchange, allow others to use your set.

Organization is a fundamental ingredient in any successful graduate career. A fat file cabinet is far better than a pile of dirty notebooks. You have an immense amount of material to keep track of, and by always maintaining a filing system you avoid many costly problems. Most universities have inexpensive photoduplication services in some of their departments, in the library, or at the student union. Use these facilities, since they are cheap and do save time.

You will find that all commentators on graduate school insist that you keep detailed and extensive files, beginning on the first day of graduate work. Even the odd professor whose office looks like a battlefield will probably have a well-stuffed filing cabinet and manila folders everywhere.

THE LIBRARY AND RELATED FACILITIES

As a graduate student, you will spend many long hours in the library. If you are working in the social sciences or humanities, you will probably consult collections of primary research materials which cannot be checked out of the library. You will also use more books than the average undergraduate does, often only glancing at some while taking short notes out of others. Thus you will discover that it is easier to read some of the materials you need in the library rather than to check them out. Students in the natural sciences are especially conscious of the time they spend in the library because they are made to read many articles in specialized journals which only the library carries and which cannot be lent out. All students find that they will have to read articles and books which are kept on reserve for their entire class to read. Besides these reasons for using the library, there is the need to do more research. For others, the library is a quiet haven for study and reading.

Since graduate students make more demands on a library's facilities than do undergraduates, familiarize yourself quickly with all of its services. As a rule, graduates are permitted to take out more books—and often for longer periods of time—than are undergraduates. They sometimes may check out materials forbidden to lower classmen. However, this usually does not apply to microfilm, microcard, and microfiche collections. If you do not know what the differences are between these three photocopy systems or how to use them, have a librarian show you. They are becoming more popular because they reduce a large amount of bulky material down to a small space. Old journals, government documents, various state, federal, and foreign government legislative records; and newspapers are being put in these film storage systems. As the years go by, students will be consulting these more often than they have in the past.

Familiarize yourself with the geography of the main library and its branches on campus. This saves you time later in finding books you cannot locate readily in the card catalogue. Be especially cognizant of where the books are kept in your field. Occasionally, walking up and down the shelves where your materials are shelved will keep you abreast of new acquisitions, and you can, at the same time, learn some bibliography by associating authors and titles with colors and shapes. Find out where the handy reference guides and bibliographies are located. Learn where the microfilm and microcard reading rooms are and where the newspapers and manuscripts are stored. Ask if your library has photoduplication facilities and where they are, and ask if the library has a photographic department that you can use. Often, such a department, for a nominal fee, will reproduce pictures, maps, and graphs for graduate students suitable for publications or for illustrating theses and dissertations.

One of the more important services available to graduate students, (and, not, as a rule, available to undergraduates) is inter-library loan (ILL). If your library does not have a book or article you need for your research, it can be ordered from another university through ILL. You go to the ILL desk and fill out a form describing the materials you want. Your library finds out if there are copies in the United States and who has them. They then borrow the material for a two or three week period and, unless the lending library forbids it, check it out to you. When the items are due, your library mails them back to the lending institution. Some libraries will charge you the cost of mailing the books, but they may only run you 20¢ to 40¢ apiece. Go ahead and spend the money: It probably is worth it. Ordinarily, plan on about three to four weeks between the time you make a request and the time when the item arrives. That it a good reason in itself to start your research early in the quarter or semester.

More likely than not, articles will be photocopied by a library and mailed to your ILL. Libraries are hesitant to send journals for fear of losing them. Your ILL librarian will probably ask how much you are willing to spend on photocopy charges. Usually, the expense is higher than on your campus, since labor costs are included. Often, your library will have a price breakdown from the lending library on duplication costs for paper copy and microfilm. This way, you can arrive at a rough idea of the possible cost to you. You may find that a long article is cheaper to order on microfilm. You should know about other ILL expenses as well. If an item is returned late or is damaged, you might be subject to fines which will probably average about what they do in your university library.

Sometimes, restrictions are placed on the use of materials. You may occasionally be prohibited from using items such as rare books or a dissertation outside your library. Other libraries may prohibit any photocopying for fear of breaking the book's spine or of violating copyright laws. Infractions of ILL rules may mean that you may not be allowed to use their services again—a privilege you would not want to lose. Also, your library could be punished by having the offended library refuse ever to lend anything to your university.

Besides ILL, you have other library conveniences. If you find that you study a great deal in the library or if you are working on a thesis or dissertation, inquire about a study carrel. These are little rooms not much bigger than a phone booth which have a desk and some shelves. The fancy ones may even have a window and a desk drawer, but do not count on it. Carrels are usually located in dark corners of the library, but the space is all yours—with a door and lock. You can leave your materials there and use your carrel whenever the library is open. Some carrels are virtually sound proof, so you can type in them. Others are open at the top, consequently you will be prohibited from using your old Underwood. If that is the case, the library probably has a room set aside where students can type within the building. To get these carrels, which are much in demand by graduate students and professors, you will have to put your name on a waiting list. If that is the case, it is never too early to sign up for one, even if, at the present, you do not think that you will want one. Later, you can tell the library that you do not need the carrel. If there is any charge for a carrel, it is usually about one dollar or less—to pay for the key—and when the key is returned, your money is refunded.

Once you have been a student for a while and have settled on a thesis or dissertation topic, you will probably find that the library is sadly lacking in key books on your project. By asking your major professor, you can usually have the library order some of this material for you. Tell your professor that you want the library to order a certain book or to buy some microfilm. Once your professor has the bibliographical information, he or she can fill out a special requisition form which goes to the library. Every department can order a certain amount of material each year in terms of dollars; and if the book budget has not already been used up, your request may be filled. If the order is big, your major professor may have to go over to the library and persuade them to pay for your material out of some other department's budget. There are always departments around that never spend all the money assigned to them, so purchasing something unusual is not necessarily difficult. But do not count on the requested material being on the shelves, bound and catalogued, within a week. If the library does purchase your requested items, it will probably take at least two months—and more likely than not, six—to get them shelved.

The same principle works with laboratory equipment. Ask your professor to see if the requested items are worth buying; if so it will take the same time and effort to obtain as books. Then hope that the items come in before you graduate. The reason for the delay is that all universities have an enormous amount of red tape to go through in order to spend money, and they are usually short-handed when it comes to doing the paper work. Some students find that it is easier to buy the book, film, or piece of equipment themselves, provided that it is not prohibitively expensive. In keeping tax records, you can always count this as a dissertation expense. For details on this point, see Chapter 2.

ACCUMULATING A LIBRARY

Living in a world of books, students find that they have to purchase some, that they want others, and that they accumulate more. Just as they need to keep note files, they should indeed collect key books in each of their fields. A small but good collection of books in their areas of specialization can prove useful in preparing for comps, in looking up information quickly, and in preparing lecture notes if they teach. Putting together a small or large library does not necessarily cost a great deal. In fact, most students pick up numerous books as well as reprints of articles and subscribe to, or have back copies of, specialized journals.

You will have to buy books for courses, and texts are expensive. Some of these you should be able to procure secondhand at the university bookstore or at other shops near campus, especially if they have been used in your course before. Bookstores near universities often have sales of monographic and technical books at reasonable prices; you should check these stores for bargains. Invariably, most campuses will have fairs or bazaars throughout the year, especially during the pleasant months of spring, to which professors and students donate books. You can find some real buys at these fairs. You might also check with the local public library for books. In many states, public libraries have to throw away books which are not checked out often enough to justify occupying valuable shelf space. Instead of destroying old volumes, some librarians will hold book sales in order to raise extra money for library expenses. These sales are always good, because what the general public might not read, you may want; and the costs often run as low as ten cents per book—and most of them are hardbacks.

From your professors, obtain the names of secondhand book dealers who publish catalogues and write to put your name on their mailing lists for free notices of their sales. By reading these immediately when you receive them, you will find bargains in your area. You have to read these quickly and order almost the same day the catalogue arrives in case the dealer only has one copy of the book. You do not want someone else to order the same item before you. Get into the habit of doing this early in your graduate career; if you are writing a thesis or dissertation requiring a great deal of book research, make it a standard practice. Dealers have many key books that you want; they will also search for specific volumes. Your major professor should be able to tell you specifically which book dealers are better for your field than others, as well as which ones are expensive and which are not. There is nothing so convenient as a personal copy of a useful book, so develop a card file on book dealers.

Other graduate students and professors sometimes unload books which you can either buy or get free. Usually, you will have to pay for books received from other students, buy you will not have to pay for books received from professors. The mid-career professors can often be seen weeding out their office libraries on slow afternoons. All through graduate school and during the first few years of teaching, the novelty of owning large numbers of books makes bibliomaniacs out of them. They also do not know what courses they will finally be teaching. After several years, they know what books they are going to be using, and they will need space for books in the area of specialization. Consequently, you may find a professor who will gladly give you a few or a dozen books in your field because they are no longer of any use. One way that is almost guaranteed to help you acquire books is to volunteer to help a professor move from one office to another. Professors often play musical chairs with their rooms, as personnel changes take place. Offer to help move books for those leaving for other campuses. During this process of moving, the professor is forced to look at books that are ordinarily never touched. Then comes the question, "Do you want these books? I don't need them any more."

Spread the word around among your friends, family, and your department that you like to collect books. It is amazing how books will reach you. Some family acquaintance, for example, may call up one day and ask if you would be interested in a couple of boxes of books. These unpredictable sources can net you some valuable materials.

One technique that graduate students have used in past years, to the point where it has become abused, is to write to publishers for free copies of their publications. If you are a TA, you may have access to departmental stationery at the same time that you have the opportunity and excuse to write to publishers asking for examination copies of their books, which you tell them are being considered as possible texts in your class.

Most publishers plan on giving away a certain number of their books as advertisement. They feel that if a professor receives a book and likes it, maybe he or she will have students purchase it. Many publishers feel that giving away one book may mean selling hundreds. Furthermore, it is a business expense which they take into account when pricing the volume.

In the past several years, the number of young professors and graduate students has increased enormously, as have the number of books—mainly texts and paperbacks—available for examination purposes. People write a publisher for one, two, or three books at a time and receive them free. Some students and professors get hundreds of books a year this way, building up their libraries at the expense of the publishing industry, with no intentions of considering using the books as texts. Some graduate students order books that they will be required to read in some courses they plan to take, thus cutting book expenses sharply.

Because this privilege has been badly abused by both students and professors, many publishers are restricting the number of volumes they give away, while others hardly send any. One popular method now in use and becoming more widespread is to send a requested book with the proviso that the professor examine it for thirty to ninety days and return it undamaged to the publishers if he or she does not require it for at least ten students. If the professor neither returns the book or orders it for the bookstore, then the publisher will send a bill, minus a professional discount of between ten and thirty percent. This has helped to cut down on the number of examination requests for some publishers and, of course, has reduced their expenses. Students using departmental stationery have been careful not to mention the fact that they were only students, consequently publishers have not been able to differentiate between professors and graduates. Since this practice is still widespread, publishers can be expected to continue restricting the flow of free copies.

University and nonprofit publishers rarely give away free books. Some state and federal agencies will. Those that do not distribute free copies will often offer a professional discount if the order is made on departmental stationery. The discount is usually about fifteen percent. Whenever you order a university press monograph you plan to pay for, try to use departmental stationery. With the costs of books today being so high, the discount can be considerable in terms of dollars saved.

The question remains, however, should you fall into the habit of writing publishers, known as "hitting," for free books? If you write occasionally for a few volumes little harm is done. But if you are abusive, you could get into trouble. Most of the larger companies have regional representatives who might be informed by the head office that a particular individual ordered fifty free books this year from them. The company asks that the salesperson check the person out. If the salesperson finds out that you are only a graduate student, not only will you never get another free book from his or her press, but you will probably have the chairman of your department reprimand you, an embarrassing situation you had best avoid. And if some publisher wants to be nasty, an editor could threaten you with some legal action in order to recover the books or their cost. This last move is very rarely made. If a student ordered books and then sold them to the bookstore as secondhand copies, a publisher might consider more than a mere reprimand, although the money involved is often too little to bother with. In order to stop this practice, many publishers now stamp each examination copy with a *Not For Resale* label which most bookstores respect. It is still cheaper for a company to scare the obnoxious person.

4
Research
And
Writing

Although many graduate programs advertise that they are not research-oriented but rather emphasize skill development, nonetheless universities are research conscious. Students see this in the requirement that faculty publish articles and books for promotions. They notice the growing library and the number of research laboratories. Students also feel research pressures in their course programs. Graduate research is usually reflected in writing papers based on work conducted in the library, on surveys among groups of people, or as a result of laboratory experiments. Whatever the means, in just about every course you register for you will have to do some writing based on far more sophisticated research than you did as an undergraduate. Yet these papers do not have to be dull and useless exercises.

You might pick a research topic that can be the subject of more than one paper for several courses. By working in one area, you will become familiar with a unique body of knowledge and its literature. Knowing a private corner of knowledge will make it easier for you quickly to pick researchable topics for term papers. Also, once the word spreads that you do most of your research around one general area, professors will hesitate to criticize your choice of papers or find fault with the final product on the assumption that you are competent to guide your own efforts. You will be carving out a new field of specialization over and above what your program offers for which there is probably no expert in the department other than yourself. You become master of a small world.

An example of what this means would help. Take, for hypothetical purposes, a Spanish language major. This student surveys the department and finds that there is no one who really knows anything about twentieth-century Spanish literature. For a course dealing with the Golden Age of Spanish literature, the student could write a paper on what influence this writing had on our century's writers. In her class on nineteenth-century Spanish literature, she could write a paper on what twentieth-century writers feel about the efforts of the past century. For the course in contemporary Spanish literature she could submit a paper on the influence of the Spanish civil war (1936–1939) on contemporary Spanish novelists. This principle can be translated into any department with some success and may eventually yield thesis and dissertation topics. A variation of this trick is to take a theme and to explore it in every paper you write, pointing it at the subject matter of the course in question.

Once you have an idea in mind for a paper, discuss it with your professor and get his approval before you start to work, even if he or she does not require you to do so. This way, if the professor has any objections, you can iron these out early, avoiding problems later. If your professor is the type who wants book reviews instead of research papers, obtain approval for the titles and ask what she or he looks for in these essays, because professors differ widely on how reviews should be done. Check with students who have taken courses under your professor to find out his or her little idiosyncrasies. You might discover, for example, that one person is a stickler for details, while another considers misspellings an original sin. Invariably, most have some weird characteristic which can easily be spotted, but check in advance anyway. Do not be afraid to ask professors about how they like their footnotes done, about whether they want bibliographies attached, and about the use of title pages. Question them about style and about what writing manual they use. Ask about how extensive the research should be or about the paper's length. But never ask these questions in class. Most professors do not like to commit themselves publicly to some hard and fast policy concerning length, depth of research, or other mechanics of the paper. See professors in their offices, where undoubtedly your chances of obtaining such information will be facilitated by privacy.

Those famous undergraduate weekend wonders are no longer usable in graduate school. Now as never before, your writing style must be as sophisticated as your extensive research, and writing style and research skills take time to develop. You must spend long hours plowing through material and then writing essays that do more than just mimic those of other authors. You must offer interesting analyses of the subjects at hand. In order to do this, you need to think; and often you need to write three or more drafts of a paper before the final copy is prepared. Start on the project early in the quarter or semester, particularly if you have more than one paper to write. Some professors even require, especially at the seminar level, papers of publishable quality to be submitted. In order to attain this level of proficiency, you will have to work hard on the project. At the risk of saying the obvious, all papers submitted in graduate school must be typed. They must have no spelling errors and only rare typographical mistakes, which must always be corrected with a black pen. Another blunder to avoid is turning in a paper late. It is just not done, and some professors will not accept tardy manuscripts. This always hurts, especially if the paper carries fifty percent of the final grade with it.

Since you will do a great deal more writing than you did as an undergraduate, keep this in mind when picking out your housing facilities. You need a little corner in this crowded world where you can spread out your notes and write papers quietly. This becomes even more imperative if you are preparing a thesis or dissertation, because you will have a great mass of material to deal with. You will not want to put away your notes each night in order to eat on the dining room table. For those writing dissertations, the ideal situation is to have a room just to yourself where you can work. If the university supplies you with an office or a library carrel, your problem may be solved. Otherwise, you may have to rent a bigger apartment or even a small house. How much room you need will depend on your own writing habits and on the quantity of materials you have to work with.

The one other problem relative to research and writing which is not widespread but which exists is plagiarism. Because of the depth of knowledge graduate professors have, it will be more difficult for a student to plagiarize in graduate school than at the undergraduate level. Professors in graduate school are constantly doing research and reading in heavier dosages than many under- graduate professors; consequently, it is often easier for them to spot plagiarism. The more senior professors are experienced in reading graduate student papers. If, all of a sudden, they receive a brilliant piece that they seem to have read before, they will be suspicious enough to check the footnotes and other sources in their well-stocked university library in order to learn whether or not the student cheated. If you are caught, not only do you flunk the course but you will never earn a degree in that department nor will you ever teach in a college or university. Any company you go to work for will want comments on you from your department, and you should realize that cheating will be mentioned. Cheating is one sin which is not tolerated at all and for which there is no forgiveness.

In recent years, companies have been formed to sell term papers, theses, and dissertations at prices running from $2.25 per page for an undergraduate paper to about $10 per page for an original dissertation. This has become a big business in the United States; many undergraduates take advantage of this service. Some graduate students will sell their old term papers to such firms for anywhere from $5 to $25 each. Others purchase papers, and there have even been some recent cases where dissertations were commissioned. Not only is this practice reprehensible from a moral point of view but in some states legal action can be brought against the student if he attends a public institution. Furthermore, the papers are expensive.

If you are going to cheat like this, why go to graduate school in the first place? Part of your education is doing research and writing. Some of the few useful things you learn in graduate school, things which you can apply in any job you go into, even if it is out of your field, are the research and writing skills you develop. Long after you have forgotten the material you memorized for tests, your researching and writing skills will still be with you. If you are planning to cheat, you should not do it in the one area where you hurt yourself the most and where you have the highest risk of being detected. This is not to say, however, that you should cheat at all in graduate school.

People do cheat in graduate school, but far less often than in undergraduate classes. Because you are older and are expected to be more responsible, plagiarism charges against you are considered far more serious than those against undergraduates, and the stigma of cheating follows you for a long time. Since this is a handbook of advice, we suggest that you have absolutely nothing to do with any of these term paper companies. The money you might make writing for them is illegal. If you write for these companies, then you can be held criminally liable in many states. Buying such papers becomes a crime if you submit them to a professor as your work.

CHOOSING M.A. AND PH.D. TOPICS

Thesis and dissertation topics are very much influenced by your major professor's inclinations and views as well as by your own thoughts on the matter. Both projects have the purpose of demonstrating that the author has research and writing abilities. Both can also be major stumbling blocks for students, since completing them requires personal initiative and varied talents.

The M.A. thesis, if it is required, does not in most cases have to be original research; rather, it may simply display research and writing skills as these are used in a specific field. Some programs require only that a seminar paper or group of papers be submitted as proof of research and writing abilities. If the latter is the case in your department, pick your term paper topics carefully and work harder on these than you otherwise might, since you will be getting double mileage out of them. Ideally, if you can select a topic which is original, then all the better.

Often the major professor will propose subjects which, in the course of his or her own work, have suggested themselves. Others will be offered by minor professors and fellow students. You will, of course, dream up some ideas. Since you may have little experience in writing these papers, it is a good idea to check with students and professors to see what they think of your latest notion. But try to settle on a topic as soon as possible in order that you may begin work on it, doing part-time research while taking courses. If you research early, you could complete your graduate work up to several months sooner.

If possible, choose a subject for which all the materials are available either on campus or quite close by. Obviously, pick something which your major professor approves. Select a topic you have some idea about, perhaps an outgrowth of a term paper. Going blindly into unknown territory could cost you time, money, and more work than you anticipated. A topic which is very broad is out of the question, and your major professor should be able to determine quickly if your proposed project is much too large. Ideally, you should grasp at some idea that can be quickly researched and written. Too many students spend an inordinate amount of time with a project that deserves less effort. In regard to length, consult your catalogue, your major professor, and the library's collection of theses. Most important, take a look at those done in your department within the past two years—and look especially at those written under your professor. This should answer your questions about length and depth of research.

At every stage of researching and writing your thesis, be in constant communication with your professor in order that he or she may guide your work. Your professor will probably make you rewrite thesis chapters several times before giving approval for the final typing. Give your readers drafts which are as clean and as stylistically sound as possible. This will mean less editorial work for a professor and may result in the completion of the thesis in a shorter time period.

Make sure that you understand the department's and the university's rules regarding preparation, format, number of copies, fees, forms, and footnote style for the thesis. As a rule , each university has a style manual which it adheres to; you must find out what it is and buy a copy. Since there are so many style books available today, it would be fruitless to list them all, especially since each school has only one it recognizes. Often the volume is listed in the department's brochure or in the general graduate school catalogue, and can be purchased in the university bookstore. Most universities have a bibliographer in the library who is responsible for making sure that theses and dissertations meet university requirements, and these individuals will not hesitate to make you retype a paper which fails to meet these standards. Retyping, unless you do it yourself, could cost one dollar per page, while the price of the local style manual is usually less than $5.

University red tape is extensive, and theses and dissertations generate paper work such as prospectuses, permits to carry on the project, library receipts for copies received, requests for graduation, departmental forms acknowledging the papers are approved: The list is endless. A month before you are to complete your degree, ask the head secretary in your department what forms you have to fill out. You might also check with the secretary at the start of your research as well. Do not waste time asking anyone else, not even the chairman of the department, because they will not be as well informed as the secretary, nor will they have copies of the forms you need.

The best guide to writing a thesis is simply to check out of the library a recently completed one from your department and to use that as your model. Also, ask your student friends in the department what has to be done. They can tell you about some of the paper work; but more important, they are in a position to comment about what influences your major professor: whether he or she is big on such things as fat footnotes, interpretation, quotes, and so on. Little bits and pieces of information of this sort can be useful to you in writing a paper which will be pleasing to your mentor.

The preparation of a dissertation is much the same as for the thesis but with several important differences. Dissertations are supposed to be the pinnacles of graduate work. They therefore must be an original contribution to knowledge. Although many do meet this requirement, in order to be original, others are written on trivial topics. The dissertation is far more important than the thesis. The former is often the basis used by colleges and universities in differentiating between several applicants for a job. This also holds true for those applying for research grants. Promotions and professional reputations are often based on the subject and quality of the dissertation, especially if the author is fortunate in having it published.

The primary task in choosing a dissertation topic is to determine if the idea you have in mind has been worked on before by other graduate students or if it has been discussed in other publications. The first place to start looking is in *Dissertation Abstracts*. This publication lists, by year, most of the dissertations done in the United States and has a master index. This is an excellent source to check in order to see if there are any dissertations done in areas related to your topic. Your professors should be able to help you next by suggesting new subjects that have never been worked on before. Check the leading journals of your subject area, since they usually list dissertations in progress. General bibliographies in your field will also be useful in settling on a topic. And if you feel that some professor is working on your idea for a book, write him and ask about his research. Chances are that you will receive a friendly, informative letter. Once you have searched and have found that no one else has your topic, then make sure that you and your major professor have a clear idea of what you will be doing.

As in the case of the master's thesis, try not to pick too broad a subject, one that may become unmanageable. Also, select one that you feel is important, since you may have to live with it for several years. Choose one which you and your professors think is publishable, even if currently you have no interest in going into print. After you finish the project, you may; and since you will have to work hard on either a good or a bad topic, you might as well try an important one.

Another factor in selecting a subject should be your skills. Obviously if you do not read Chinese, a dissertation on eighteenth-century Chinese poetry by you would be a disaster. Pick a project which you feel you are good at and can handle intellectually. If you like researching abnormal psychology, avoid writing outside that area. If you enjoy diplomatic history, do not write on cultural topics. By finding a topic you can manage because of your background, you will have an easier time in applying for research funds, since your record will give the grant people some confidence in your ability to complete the project.

If you can select a dissertation subject which can be researched on campus or with a minimum of travel, this is advisable. You will save a fortune in travel expenses and in time lost in going from one place to another. You will have the convenience of working when you want without the pressure of slaving long hours simply to take advantage of a short stay at some library. Picking a topic that relates to, or is an outgrowth of, your M.A. thesis is a popular method used, since it gives the student a head start of the research, much of which will already have been done in the local university library. You save time, since by then you will know almost exactly what other research you need to do and probably what new chapters you will need to write. If you choose an idea unrelated to your M.A. thesis, pick it as early as possible in order to start part-time research while you are still taking courses. This also gives you time to develop your thoughts before committing them to paper.

In recent years, the tendency has been to reduce the length of the dissertation. Literature people, for example, who wrote up to 800 page dissertations in the 1940s, can now write only 300 pages. This trend is evident in all branches of knowledge. Your major professor, will, no doubt, give you some idea of the expected length of the dissertation; your research will be another determining factor. Remember as you write that the longer the dissertation, the more it will cost to have it typed and duplicated. If it is too long, a publisher will want you to cut it. There is no general rule of thumb that one can go by; you simply have to see how long dissertations are in your field and then decide how much you want to write. Because so many people are writing dissertations today, duplication of a project has become more common. In order to protect yourself, try to research your subject in such a way that you can write it up in one of several fashions. Your major professor can be more specific on this point. And if you have more material than you really want to use, save some for future publications. There is no law that says that everything you dig up has to go into the manuscript.

SPECIAL PROBLEMS WITH THESES AND DISSERTATIONS

Thesis and dissertation stages of graduate work are far different from course portions and require special character and personality traits to complete them. Writing stages in graduate school prove to be stumbling blocks for too many students. There are no precise statistics on this, but in every department there can be found those who had no difficulties taking courses and comps, but who somehow never finished their theses, or more common, their dissertations. Often the problem is money. A student goes to work after exams, planning to raise money for research, and never does it. Another might not have the time to prepare a dissertation while working. But others never finish simply because they lack the self-discipline it takes. If a major reason for not completing the degree has to be chosen, it would be this character deficiency.

Essentially, the person who comes to graduate school is a professional at taking courses and does well in them. In classes, after about six years of experience, most students can handle all the assignments, completing them within the prescribed time. But all these tasks are short-term in nature, and the student is put on a timetable by a professor or by a school calendar. Then this student is exposed all of a sudden to something different: a long term project in which he or she sets the pace, goals, and schedule. For many, this is a new experience which they cannot cope with easily unless they have a major professor who pushes them all the way through to completion.

What the student comes up against are such problems as determining how much time will be devoted to research and discovering where to do it. Then there are other questions developing: How long should the writing take; how much time should be spent organizing notes; how many pages a day should be produced? To compound things, researching and writing a large project like this takes some real organizational abilities. You must decide how to go about the research, how you will organize your notes, and how you will block out your chapters. Fortunately, your major professor will usually be able to make valuable time-saving suggestions which may spare useless efforts of your own. Often the professor's comments will make sense, since he or she has seen mistakes before and has probably made a few of them.

You need to decide how long you are going to write and set up a timetable to live by, revising it only when it appears that the original plan was unrealistic. If it calls for you to wake up at eight in the morning, research for six hours, and write five pages a day, do it religiously, never breaking your schedule. You will find students who say that they do their best work when inspiration hits them rather than in the manner just suggested. They are telling you a fairy tale; they are the ones who will not finish their dissertations. That may work for a term paper or for a book review, both of which are short, but that technique will not apply to a long project. Ask those around you who have just finished, or who are putting the last touches on a dissertation, how they did it and you will probably find that the theme is organization with a timetable. The important thing is to develop a schedule you can keep all the way to the end.

The efficiency gained in this way will save you time. Your professor will be able to read your chapters at a comfortable pace, and with your self-imposed unofficial deadline before your next one is ready, you will find that drafting will come more quickly and that the project will stay "hot" all the way to its conclusion. Rewriting chapters for your professor should also be worked into your schedule as well, perhaps between the time you finish the first draft of a chapter and start on another. This is something you will have to work out on your own and with your professor.

There is one other advantage to organization. If you have decided, for example, to write five pages each day, when you finish your quota, your work is done. You can go to the movies or to a party that night without any worry, since you are on schedule. In contrast, the student who has no master plan will always worry about whether he or she is doing enough work. And although in fact his level of productivity may be greater than that of others, such a student will not realize it.

Once you have completed writing your dissertation and your professor has smiled with approval, plan on spending about two months more working with the manuscript. During this period, you will have to make your committee read the paper, and that alone will take up a great deal of your time, even when you urge them to work quickly. More days will be spent having the final copy typed, either by yourself, a friend, or a professional typist. Then there is the matter of making copies for your professor, the library, University Microfilms (which will put it on film as a permanent file), and yourself. There is proofreading to be done and an oral defense to go through. Trying to find a time when the entire committee can meet for your defense is not so easy, what with classes to teach and meetings to attend. All of these activities cost you time.

An efficient and experienced major professor can anticipate many of the problems you will have and should be able to help you through the more difficult portions of your work. Many students feel that the dissertation period of their graduate career is the most enjoyable, but a poor choice of professors or a lack of organization can make your work difficult, disconcerting, and unproductive.

OFF-CAMPUS RESEARCH

The discussion on off-campus research will be limited to the use of other libraries, because non-library investigation is subject to too many variables to comment about profitably. Most students doing off-campus work will, in all likelihood, consult other libraries or regional, state, and federal archives. Or they may travel to other countries to gather their materials. This is especially true for social science and humanities students. Extensive work at other libraries is necessary only for dissertations, but thesis students and those working on research papers will often avail themselves of these other facilities.

The better your preparation is before you leave campus to do research, the quicker and more efficient will be your work in other libraries. Find out as much as possible about your topic before you start traveling. Consult bibliographic guides and professors to determine what other libraries have that you need to consult. And if you are doing research in libraries outside of the United States, write their head librarians to find out what kind of paper work you have to go through before permission is granted to consult their holdings. Some will require letters of introduction from your university, others request that you file a formal plea to use their resources, and a few can only be used once you have found someone who has enough influence to get you inside.

Once you have determined that a given collection of material (usually manuscripts) is rich in information, have the items you want photocopied or microfilmed if this is permitted, because it will probably be cheaper than paying hotel and restaurant expenses while you laboriously take notes. Do this also in foreign countries. In some libraries, especially those outside the United States, you will not have access to filming facilities, and therefore there is nothing else to do but plant yourself in a chair and take notes. If you can order filming, you may be able to arrange to have the materials shipped to you and be billed for them once you are back at your home campus. This way, you can save your cash to pay hotel, food, and transportation expenses. Most libraries in the United States, and a large number outside the country, are very cooperative with visiting scholars and students and will go out of their way to accommodate your needs. To them, it is a compliment that you have need of their services. Furthermore, no library wants to develop a bad reputation if it can be avoided.

Some students find that the best time to make trips for term paper and dissertation material is during quarter and semester breaks. They leave campus for about a week, which is probably all they can afford anyway, visiting neighboring libraries, taking notes, photocopying and microfilming, checking what these facilities have, and then returning to campus with enough materials to work with for the next several months. If you plan your term papers far enough in advance, you can produce some excellent manuscripts based on impressive research that really took little effort. This technique is used by professors who cannot leave campus while they are teaching but who want to do research. And if your trips are planned properly, you may even be able to make advance arrangements to stay in a dorm at some other campus for nothing or for about a dollar per night. You could also plan to spend a few nights with a friend. Besides, a week or just a few days away from your campus, for whatever reason, is a vacation.

Although many graduate students will never feel the need to leave campus to do research, there are those who will. Developing a familiarity with other major libraries is a good habit. You never know when such information may be useful in your work or in advising someone else. One other point in regard to other libraries: Whenever you are traveling, especially if by car, visit major libraries that you pass. The stop will be a welcome rest from driving, and you may find a collection useful to your own work which you otherwise might have missed. And the cost in time can be negligible, even if you don't find a gold mine of interesting material. After a few years, your knowledge of neighboring libraries will be quite extensive, and other students and professors will be coming to you for specific information regarding them. Needless to say, this does wonders for your reputation within the department.

WHY PUBLISH?

In the past several years, the number of Ph.D.s awarded in the United States has outstripped the availability of jobs that doctoral students traditionally sought, and the present economic crunch is making prospects even more dismal. The result is that competition for the lessening number of open positions, especially in teaching, is increasing considerably. This condition is forcing many graduate students to reconsider what they can offer prospective employers. Such traditional qualifications as a finished or near-finished Ph.D., good grades, well-rounded programs, favorable letters of recommendation, teaching or working experience, and so on are often no longer sufficient to guarantee success in the job market. One obvious way in which a graduate student can make his or her job application more appealing than the others in the seven-inch pile on the employer's desk is to include a list of several scholarly publications.

In the past, many graduate students have been hesitant to publish their work, feeling that it was not worthy enough or that many journals would refuse to consider their efforts. Often students do significant research and writing—indeed, they are compelled to do so for their programs—and in this respect they have a definite advantage over older scholars who are not always pressured to produce. Obviously, too, some graduate research is suitable for publication. Because many graduate students are publishing today, questions have been raised about the student's role within the academic structure. This creates problems for both students and faculty. Students have always led a dual existence as both pupils and neophyte scholars, but they have previously stressed the former. Today, the emphasis is slowly shifting. Many graduate students are devoting a growing amount of time and effort to publishing, thus tending to undermine the traditional role of the graduate student. And for this reason, some of the negative aspects of publishing should be mentioned so that you can decide whether or not to publish.

Numerous individuals, either on their own initiative or through the encouragement of a faculty member, elect to complete their graduate education at a slower pace, hoping that the job situation will improve and allowing time for additional research and writing in their own fields. Conversations with graduate students from many universities indicate that this situation may lessen the importance of the graduate program itself and increase the significance of publications in the eyes of the student. If this is true, it is possible that even narrower specialists will be produced in American graduate schools. Programs themselves have not changed much in the recent past, but students' attitudes toward them have. For example, many Ph.D. students are not devoting as much attention to their minor fields; instead, they concentrate an ever increasing amount of time to publishing in their major field. The rationale is that a list of publications in the major area is more important than a distinguished academic record in other fields. Some argue that if they have published, a minor professor would not, indeed should not, be too concerned about their performance on such traditional academic hurdles as comps. There are still many students, however, who consider course work more important than writing, but their ranks appear to be thinning. At any rate, disagreement among students over the need to publish sometimes generates the same hostility that this topic has traditionally caused among faculty members.

Student-faculty relationships are also undergoing changes, in part because of the publishing student. Some major professors encourage their students to publish; others do not. If a student wishes to publish and has a major professor who is more concerned with the formal graduate program, conflicts occur. On the other hand, if a student does not wish to publish but has a professor who encourages it, the situation is even worse. Doing more than is expected is not as great a sin as doing less. In the case of the student who devotes considerable time to writing, relationships with minor professors are often strained because their fields do not receive the same careful attention that they would under other circumstances. The miffed minor professor might give poor grades and consider failing the student on the comprehensive exams.

Aside from discord between the student and minor professors, occasionally there is difficulty between the student and other academicians. For example, problems develop when students publish more than some young faculty members. This can lead to disrespect on the part of the student and can make young teachers feel uncomfortable in their relationships with these students. In addition, professors who see themselves as "teachers" as opposed to "researchers" may feel the urge to teach the aggressive student a lesson in humility. A student who is sensitive to these concerns can, with tact, diffuse some of this natural resentment.

Publishing students also create stress in faculty relationships. A major professor may feel a certain pride in having such a student and might be more willing than in other cases to shield the student from the criticisms of minor professors, even though he or she is well aware that the student has neglected the minor areas. The professor who is more concerned with the student's performance in his or her field than with the student's publications in another often resents the "mother hen" attitude of the major professor. Although protecting one's students has always been a common practice, the publishing mania among students appears to be causing this to be even more pronounced, creating even greater tensions among faculty members. This is not to say, of course, that such tendencies are new, but simply that they may be on the increase.

The stress and conflict caused by the publishing student may not be worth all of the anxiety. Students usually publish hoping to improve their chances in the job market, which holds true for university positions. However, since there are few university openings today, the student will have to look at two- and four-year colleges or at industry and government for jobs. These may shy away from applicants who have published because, their recruiters claim, scholars interested in research may not devote enough effort to teaching or to working. This is most pronounced if the student is applying to junior colleges where administrators may even be reluctant to hire Ph.D.s, not to mention ones with publications.

This forces the student to question the value of publishing. If you are going to publish, be aware of these negative points. If you elect not to publish, you may be able to complete graduate work earlier than if you do; but you will also reduce your chances of securing some jobs. A few publications may be the ideal for students. It shows that the student has initiative and that he or she can publish; it also suggests that other concerns, such as studying and teaching, also play an important role. And a few publications will not cost you so much time that you will delay graduating. You must be aware of the positive and negative aspects of publishing before launching into what could be dangerous waters.

HOW TO PUBLISH

The first hurdle in publishing is to pick a publishable subject for required research papers. This same consideration should be primary in the choice of a thesis or dissertation topic. Of immediate concern, particularly for research papers, should be the availability of significant material in the student's library. Few editors are interested in considering a graduate student's view on some well-worn subject. Furthermore, they will seldom consider an article on a narrower topic on which some work has already been published. You should also avoid choosing a subject of a trivial and insignificant nature.

A practical approach is to begin by picking a specific journal toward which to slant your work. Consider the type of materials it prints, its footnote policy, and the suggested length for articles; then write your required paper not so much for the professor as for the journal. More often than not, professors do not object to this procedure. After the instructor has returned the paper to you, hopefully with helpful comments both on style and content, it can be converted into a publishable item. Of course, this also applies to thesis chapters. Quite often, very little additional work is necessary to convert a good research paper or thesis chapter into an article. Another source of article material is leftover thesis research. Often while writing the thesis, a student collects a great deal of material which is not included in the finished product. When properly exploited, such research can result in one or more publications.

Choosing a journal for one's first publication is crucial. Sending your first article to *Playboy* will probably result in a wounded ego. The top magazines and journals are very competitive: Hundreds of articles are rejected by each every year. You should keep in mind the element of competition. State and topical journals on the other hand, because of their narrower scope and more specialized readership, are more receptive to the type of articles generally produced by graduate students. Local journals, university publications, and association magazines should also be investigated as possible outlets. University journals are rapidly growing in number and are published as vehicles for faculty research. Often such periodicals will consider work by graduate students. Most of these are not restricted to any particular field but accept papers from many disciplines, including yours.

Some students, at one time or another, do research pertaining to countries other than the United States. Therefore, foreign journals should be considered. They are generally less competitive than those in the United States, and they welcome articles from American scholars. Many foreign journals publish in more than one language, thus making an article in English acceptable. In order to determine whether or not a particular journal will publish in English, consult *Ulrich's International Periodicals Directory* or simply write the editor of the journal you have in mind. If you write well in another language, the number of foreign journals in which you can publish is vastly increased. Even if you cannot compose in a foreign language, the problem is not insurmountable. For example, you can have a foreign language graduate student translate the article. You should include the translator on the title page as co-author or pay him for the service. It should be noted, as an added inducement, that many foreign scholarly journals pay their contributors while few American ones do.

You could also consider publishing in journals outside your field in related areas. The critical factor is the subject of the manuscript. If you have an article that fits into two fields, consider journals from both. Some welcome this type of article as it allows them to claim that they are an interdisciplinary publication transcending the artificial boundaries of knowledge. Although most of the time this is just pure propaganda, people in other fields often have unique and valuable views of other areas. This factor could possibly make one of your articles even easier to publish in an important journal outside your field than in one in your area.

No matter what type of journal you are considering, certain rules of etiquette should be observed. Have the courtesy to look through the specific journal you have in mind in order to ensure that your topic is not totally unsuitable. If you are in doubt on this particular point, write the editor describing your idea. The editor would much rather read an inquiring letter than be forced to reject a good manuscript on an unsuitable subject.

When communicating with an editor, and particularly while submitting a manscript, always explain who you are, where you are studying, and whether or not you have published before. This will save the editor the trouble of having to write inquiring about your academic status if he or she decides to accept your manuscript. Even if you are a beginning M.A. student, say so. Theoretically at least, this is not held against you. Above all, do not attempt to "snow" editors; they know you are not Albert Einstein or Margaret Mead.

Most periodicals state some basic requirements for submitting manuscripts, usually on the inside cover. Be courteous enough to comply in all particulars. For example, if these instructions say to send two copies of the paper, do so. Others may require that you send a self-addressed stamped envelope for returning your paper if it is rejected. It is a good policy to enclose return postage in any case. Always observe the footnote style of the journal to which you are submitting your article. There is no excuse for failing to comply. Failure to do so may give a stuffy editor an excuse to reject your contribution.

Certain basic rules should also be followed in the physical preparation of the manuscript. Use an electric typewriter if at all possible, it is neater. Double-space everything, including the extended footnotes and quotes. Place the footnotes at the end of the manuscript, and do not include a bibliography unless the journal calls for one. Since appearance may be an influencing factor, do not submit a paper with typographical errors. Preferably, use quality, nonerasable bond. Proofread your manuscript carefully; you cannot expect an editor to accept a poorly typed paper. One should always keep a copy of the final draft because some are lost in the mail, and occasionally editors are careless.

After you submit an article, do not pester the editor. Most editors acknowledge receipt of the manuscript immediately; others do not. The editor will notify you as soon as a decision has been made about your contribution. Processing an article takes time, anywhere from a month to a year. Ordinarily, however, a decision is rendered in about three months. In addition, if your article is accepted, do not expect immediate publication. This may take from a few months to several years, depending on the journal's backlog.

Quite often, an editor will propose certain changes in the article. The wise author complies with his suggestions. Although it is your work, it is his magazine. More often than not, these suggestions pertain to minor grammatical and stylistic matters. Rarely does an editor attempt to change the meaning or content of your manuscript. If the editor feels that fundamental changes are necessary, he will probably reject the article outright.

The editor usually sends the author either galley or page proofs of the article. These should be read and corrected immediately. Do not attempt to rewrite parts of the article once it is in proof. Not only does this irritate the editor and printer, but it may hold up publication of the entire issue. Further, resetting of type may be billed to you. The only changes the author should make are corrections of printer's errors. Mail back the proofs within three days. Some magazines will not offer the author a chance to correct proofs. In this case, all that you can do is hope the paper will be printed to your satisfaction. After publication, the editor will send you a varying number of reprints of your article, several copies of the journal, or both. If you get reprints, give one to each person who helped you on the article; and, of course, your major professor should receive an autographed copy.

Having once published in a particular journal, do not flood the beleaguered editor with everything you write. Chances are that if you submit one good article to him, an editor will be inclined to accept a second one in the future. But do not overwork one journal. When you produce other manuscripts, remember that there are other magazines.

Although graduate students rarely publish books, it does happen. It is more difficult for a student to have a book published than an article. However, finding a publisher and having the book published are done much the same way as for an article. Rarely is a thesis worthy of full publication, and hardly ever does a student have time to research and write a long manuscript. If you try to write a book, remember that it is difficult to publish and that the time you spend could hurt your studying. But whether you publish an article or a book, do the best job you can, even if it takes time. You do not want a bad manuscript published where the whole world can see your incompetence. Five years from now, you will want to look back at the paper and still be able to say that you did a good job. And since your later reputation may be based solely on your publications, a bad article can hurt.

5
Graduate Life

SPECIAL PROBLEMS
OF THE FEMALE STUDENT

The special problems besetting female graduate students are both obvious and subtle. Although a woman seeking recognition as a construction worker often faces blatant opposition and resentment, her sister in academia appears to have an easier time of it. Liberal male intellectuals who pride themselves on sex-blindness are more slippery prey, because prejudices against women can often be justified by defining them either as personality conflicts or as incompetence on the part of a female. Yet both male and female graduate students and many professors acknowledge that there is much discrimination against the woman student, despite the efforts of the United States Government to correct this by its use of education funds.

On December 31, 1971, the *Washington Post* reported that the Equal Opportunity Commission found massive prejudice against women in colleges and universities. During the same month, Ethel Bent Walsh reported to the American Association of Science that "a massive, consistent and vicious pattern of sex discrimination" existed, a pattern demonstrated by requiring higher grade point averages for entering females in graduate schools, by unfair partiality toward men in granting aid, and through the reluctance of some professors to take on new female students. Yet this prejudice is not limited to the natural and physical sciences. To varying degrees, this problem is still with us in all disciplines. It permeates every area of study and can be found in all graduate schools, far more often than at the undergraduate level. The problem is so great that the Department of Health, Education, and Welfare considers women as a minority group when stipulating to a university what percentages of Blacks, Chicanos, and other minorities must be enrolled or hired in order for the university to receive Federal aid. In many cases, female graduate students and professors are sought after much as one seeks a token Black—to satisfy a quota system only.

Although this prejudice exists, one should not be under the impression that there are no graduate students who welcome female peers or that there are no professors who want women for students. Quite to the contrary, most departments have people who are comfortable with female colleagues. If you are a woman, it may be necessary to avoid those who dislike female students and to hope that the others will help protect you from the blatant prejudice, at least in the granting of assistantships and fellowships.

In order to help combat these problems, a woman must come to graduate school equipped to answer certain stock questions dealing with her marital status, her plans for motherhood, and her career. She must ask herself why she "really" came to graduate school and what, if anything, she proposes to do with her education. Does she plan to teach, go into industry, or marry and raise a family? You will be asked about these points within the first twenty-four hours you are on campus. Have some responses worked out. Vague answers will be met with chuckles and knowing, fatherly looks which soon grate on your nerves. Try to make friends with the one or more faculty members who will treat you as an individual rather than as a sex object. The other female students, if there are any, will quickly point out the department's bigots. Having faculty allies is important, because you will need someone to defend you in faculty meetings and at bull sessions and parties. Armed with some answers and some allies, you can face any other obstacles that will confront you.

Knowing why you are in graduate school is a comfort for those times when self-doubt invades your mind or when some professor gives you a hard time. Despite ambition, a few professors still do not take women seriously, and others find faults in them that they would let pass in a man. In arguments, some women are brushed aside as hysterical females. You find that although pursuing an intellectual career in the man's world of academia does not require you to alter such personal habits as dress, hobbies, and speech patterns, you have to achieve a delicate balance between good manners, thoroughness, hard work, and, above all, aggressiveness. Being confident of your goals helps your balance.

Sexual stereotypes, as well as sexual proprieties, often stand between a woman and success in graduate school, and later in the academic world. When women act in traditionally feminine ways—sweet, yielding, soft-spoken—male professors like them as individuals. But competition is fierce in graduate school, and often the only trait that differentiates between the mediocre and the successful student is an aggressive character. Unfortunately, the gentleman scholar would much prefer the quiet young lady. This is particularly true with senior teachers and becomes more evident in the older and more tradition-soaked departments, disciplines, and universities.

The average female graduate student will have some difficulty in finding a major professor. Often these male teachers do not want to spend time working with a woman because they find it hard to see them as colleagues. As her male peers will probably point out to her, most of the senior professionals, and this includes many important members of the department, would rather work with male graduate students. Because the major professor is so crucial, the female may find it advisable to find a mentor among the ranks of the younger professors who may be more inclined to deal with her in the same fashion as a male student. As with any major decision on school, check with both your female and male friends in order to determine if the particular young professor is likely to pose any problems. It may not be worthwhile, for example, to have the local Casanova-in-residence as your major professor.

Sex has its problems even beyond classes. A great deal of the education one receives comes from outside the lecture hall, in professor's offices, over cups of coffee, on research trips, and at other informal situations. Since mose professors are men, women are often shut out of this type of communication because it just would not look right for a bright, young, married Ph.D., for example, to be seen frequently in a bar having a beer with a pretty co-ed or to have it known that a certain woman spends hours in someone's locked office. Professors expect to stay in the department long after you are gone, and some fear being grist for the gossip machine. One thing you will soon learn is that professors and students are just as gossipy as any other group and that people govern their lives accordingly.

If a generalization has to be made, it is that women will find less prejudice among fellow students than among the faculty. Few males today will openly complain that women are grabbing up slots or assistantships within their department. That complaint will be registered when they start looking for jobs. As a consequence of decreased sexist prejudice among students, you will find that you can make friends with male students in your department. They will most likely be willing to help you with advice on how to negotiate each of graduate school's hurdles. Then there is always the odd student who virtually snarls when women come around; but pay no attention to him, his colleagues already know he is weird.

You will find another set of problems outside the department. Often, the first year in graduate school is also a woman's first year away from either home or dormitory. You must learn to deal with the whole male-oriented arrangement that combines your safety with freedom to study in peace, or in your finding a part-time job that does not interfere with your school work. Fortunately, there are many women's organizations already in existence to help you with some of these problems, and more organizations spring up all the time. Every campus today has a women's association which not only becomes involved in the women's movement but which also has more immediate value in that it can guide people to housing and even to jobs. In your community, various women's clubs can also help you adjust to your new surroundings. If you have problems, check with your female friends and professors, with graduate students, or with the student union for the name of the women's group on campus. They are usually so well organized that even if you have marital difficulties or face crude forms of job and academic discrimination their influence can be useful.

You need to keep in mind that your goal in graduate school should be to do well academically and to move on with the degree(s) into whatever career you want. In order to do this, you will sometimes have to ignore subtle forms of prejudice. If you let what really are petty disturbances irritate you, professors will lash back, possibly prejudicing your chances of completing graduate school. This is a harsh but true fact of life, and there is no real alternative for you other than to quit. Then again, you may be lucky and not have to face such problems where you attend school, but do not count on it.

ARRIVAL ON CAMPUS

Relations among graduate students, although similar in many ways to undergraduate associations, undergo changes at the graduate level, due in large part to the wide variety of student ages and backgrounds. Students may range from their twenties into the not so uncommon fifties. Not only do they come from every corner of the United States and from many parts of the world, but often you find students who have worked after earning their B.A. who have spent several years in the armed services, or who have attended other graduate schools. Consequently, these various ages and experiences affect their points of view on many subjects. Their attitudes toward studying are more serious than ever, and their level of productivity increases from undergraduate days. An ever growing number of students in graduate school are married and have children. Their job desires are more explicit than at the undergraduate level. In short, graduate students are more mature and serious than their undergraduate counterparts. They should be treated with respect as a whole since they can help you with practical advice and can prove to be interesting company.

One of the central themes of this book is the emphasis placed on graduate students as one of your best sources of information about graduate programs. When you first arrive on campus, seek them out to find where the department is located and to find information about courses, about expenses, and about the university town in general. No one volunteers this information; you will have to ask for it. Students are knowledgable about such things as the program structure, the requirements, the difficulties and talents of specific professors, and the quality of the courses. They are walking encyclopedias about graduate life, far more so, it would sometimes appear, than your professors. At least students will talk more honestly with you than many professors. Always consult students in your department because graduate students in other departments know little or nothing about your program. You might also see more than one student on a given question, since there may be a discrepancy of information. You should also consult professors to get their views, especially regarding the university town.

Since in a sense you are a freshman again when you arrive at a new campus, you will have to ask an inordinate number of questions. Students will help with honest advice and will not try to deceive you. They understand that one of the ways to complete graduate work successfully is by mutually helping each other along. A word of warning, however: A graduate student, will, more often than not, defend his or her major professor. If you hear good things about a professor, check it out with another student.

Although the kind of questions you can ask a fellow student may sound obvious to you, they bear repeating here, especially for incoming graduate students. You should find out what courses each professor teaches in the department and what their work requirements and grading policies are. You may discover that three different people teach a particular class and that two of them do it horribly. F½ind out what it is like to major under the various people you have in mind. No doubt several short conver-stations on this point will rapidly reduce your list of potential mentors. Ask about how many hours and about what courses must be taken for each of the various fields. This is important since programs are always undergoing many changes, some of which may not have crept into departmental or university publications. This is becoming even more the case, since programs usually change in the spring for the fall session. There are always hidden, unpublished requirements, such as the specific languages they accept and the sequence in which professors want courses taken. You should be fully aware of these revisions, because faculties are notorious for making major changes in a program without consulting or even informing their students. Although your program can be fully governed by the catalogue under which you entered school, you may find the new changes to your advantage. Before deciding to stick to the old catalogue require-ments or going with the new, understand all the changes.

With regard to housing, first check with students if you have not made prior arrangements. Professors can be of only secondary help, since many of them live in houses rather than in apartments near the university. Take advantage of your conversations to find out about shopping centers, state residency requirements, food stamps, and welfare programs. Some students even find they qualify for welfare and food stamps!

Hopefully, you will be arriving on campus several days before registering for classes. Check both with the secretary in your department and with fellow students on how to register, since this ancient ritual varies with each school. Your graduate courses will rarely be closed out, but do not take chances. Some professor may be a super popular instructor teaching a course you want, and unless you can preregister or obtain a class card in advance, you may not get into that class. In order to avoid difficulties with registration, as well as with other activities occupying your time during these early days, ask about the campus geography and procure the university's handy campus map.

If there is a coffee room in the department, or even if you have to gather a group of students together elsewhere, do so in order to find out what their attitudes are toward the department and the universtiy. In this way, you can quickly find out such things as what the morale problems, if any, are, what the general tone of behavior is, what cliques exist in your department, and what people do not like each other. Once you find this out, avoid taking sides in any of these cliques, or at least do not do so until you fully understand what the consequences might be.

YOUR IMAGE

How to win friends and influence people is a subject more aptly handled by a Dale Carnegie; but since one's image in a department can be a factor determining success in graduate school, some of the more obvious points may help. One's impression of fellow students is also important since they will be future colleagues who may hire you, help your students, publish or review your books, or recommend you for academic honors. And, of course, they will be friends for many years.

During the first few months on campus, you will need to work harder than anyone else. Have all your assignments done before their deadlines. This means that all your efforts must also show the best quality you are capable of and that the work should be done with a sense of efficiency. If you are collaborating with some other student on a project, do your share and then some. If you promise to look something up for someone or to bring in materials you own, do it promptly so that you soon gain a reputation for being quick, competent, and reliable. Throughout these early months, become familiar with the journals in your field and read book reviews, comments on meetings, and general bibliographic essays so that you can participate in other graduate students' conversations. Since professors and students talk shop more often than not, reading a professor's articles and reviews of his or her books and learning about what goes on in your major field is all-important in commanding respect for your professional abilities.

Every major field has a national association which usually admits students to membership at reduced rates. Join as soon as possible; read their journal and blurbs in order to discuss professional activities with the people around you. There are some other advantages with membership. Besides the journal, many scholarly organizations charter airplanes for travel in and outside of the United States at highly reduced rates. You can attend their conventions as a member and have as much fun at these as you would at any other industry's meetings. Your name and address appears on a membership list which is available to all other members, and you never know if someone will write you to offer their help on one of your research projects.

Read everything you can find that has been written by your professors. Do this to protect yourself by knowing what their views and professional interests are. Also, it is flattering to them when you casually mention one of their publications in the course of conversation. Talking to them about their books and articles will give you an idea about their nonacademic opinions on many subjects. Since many students do not even read their major professor's publications, you will quickly become a source of information for others who are seeking your assessment of various faculty members.

Volunteering for what may seem the hard way to do things can pay off. For example, when oral reports are being assigned, offer to present your report first or at least early in the course. This makes you appear as an eager student, but more important, it means that you get a nuisance assignment out of the way, thus leaving time for other projects. You might also consider registering for courses which students consider difficult. You will probably learn a great deal, since the workload tends to be higher and the professors more competent than in normal or easy classes. Remember that there are many graduate students who are passive and who take the line of least resistance. If you avoid that tactic and show some initiative, the chances of working well with these more active students and the more competent professors are good.

The whole purpose of these suggestions is to encourage your professors to start regarding you almost as an equal as soon as possible. Gaining respect from your peers and professors gives you more flexibility in what you study and how you study; it allows you to influence attitudes and, possibly, to shape the very structure of the program. When reforms come up for discussion, people may turn to you for advice. There is nothing like being able to convert your peers to views you have nurtured and then see your ideas converted into remodeled programs. Few faculty members like rabble-rousers, but most respect responsible innovators.

In your drive for respect, avoid belittling any particular student or professor, either to his face or behind his back. With gossip running rampant in your department, the less you say which is of a derogatory nature the better for you. Eschew acting superior in front of your peers as well. There are too many snobs in graduate school already and they are despised as much as anywhere else. If anything, try to be helpful by offering advice on how to solve research and study problems, by making suggestions for thesis and dissertation topics, by sharing your materials, by critiquing papers, and by sharing research.

Publishing is another means of increasing your stock in the department. But, as suggested in the previous chapter, this can be a double-edged sword. Since publishing articles and books is considered one of the goals of academia, letting students know you indulge in the fun of writing is important, but it must be done with discretion. Often you will find that both publishing and nonpublishing students can help you in your work by offering research and writing advice. Their active participation will make them aware of your efforts without your having to advertise, and they will undoubtedly let everyone else know what you are doing. Do the same with professors by consulting them on research and writing. They will ask what you are publishing and how much you have done before. These professors, in turn, will tell other colleagues about your work. The result is that your fame grows with little effort on your part.

There is also an image of the ideal scholar which you should understand. A scholar is idealized by many as a humble, hard working, calm individual who never becomes excited about a new publication, receiving it and all points of view concerning it with reserved detachment. A scholar is supposed never to be biased or irrational. Therefore, a scholar's colleagues pay attention to what he or she says, including such a person's comments on your performance.

Some students, especially new ones, tend to make some serious social mistakes. For example, there is always the individual who brags about his undergraduate school. If you went to an important college, everyone will soon find out about it anyway. Then there is the person who earns a reputation for living in the department's lounge drinking coffee all day and blowing hot air on any subject. Nobody likes an opinionated stuffed shirt or a lazy student.

It is also wise to maintain a formal reserve with your professors until you learn how familiar to be with them. You might also try to maintain middle-of-the-road dress styles. Whether you are in school or out on the street, people still judge you by your appearance, and there is no need to alienate people simply because of a few clothes. Although you know from your undergraduate days that many professors do not care how students dress, some are irritated by unusual fashions.

The question of whether or not all these various tactics directed at expanding your reputation are merely truckling to professors is a legitimate one. At the high school or college level, "brown-nosing" a teacher or professor is considered a dishonest way to earn good grades. If you do this in graduate school for the same reason, the same holds true. There is no substitute for excellence. Yet answering test questions well and writing clever papers does not tell a professor enough about you. They need to know you well in order to advise you and, later, to help you find a job. Further, with so many highly gifted students around, stiff competition forces you to find some means of making yourself stand out, especially when you are applying for scholarships and jobs.

PROFESSIONAL ORGANIZATIONS

Although some mention has already been made about professional organizations, you should keep in mind that these groups do play an important part in your academic life. By joining the one or two important ones, you can keep up with news concerning fellowships, grants, jobs, and conventions. Besides the monographic journal that usually comes with membership, there is often a much more useful newsletter, published either as part of the journal or in separate form. Many of these societies print bibliographies of new publications and research currently in progress. Once you have an idea of what your dissertation will be on, you can use these tools to determine if someone else is already working on your topic and to broadcast your topic conveniently to everyone in the profession as a declaration of implied ownership. These organizations also publish membership lists with addresses which you can use in writing to other people in your field, should the need arise. And if you are listed in the membership list or in a bibliography of current research, you may receive unexpected help in your work from some obscure corner of the country.

Student membership in a professional organization usually costs between $5 and $15 per year. Consider this part of your education expenses, like tuition. If you eventually teach or work in a related area, you will want to continue your membership. You can sometimes save money in travel expenses after being a member for at least six months. Using one example, the American Historical Association charters dozens of airplanes each summer to fly professors and students all over Europe to do research. Political scientists, archeologists, and natural and physical scientists, among others, also need to travel in the United States and overseas and they often do so through various professional organizations.

BUILDING A PROFESSIONAL REPUTATION

Some students have no interest in planning for the day when they must leave graduate school. For those who eventually want to enter the academic profession—the goal of most graduate students—or for those who wish to enter a closely related field, such as research work, it is possible to develop the reputation within your profession that is so vital for a successful career. With just a small effort, you can do this while you are still a graduate student. Belonging to a professional organization is, of course, the first and easiest step.

A second move is to do some publishing. This quickly spreads your name around, since people will glance at your articles, others will receive copies, and the rest will see them listed in bibliographies of current publications. Publishing is, in fact, your best medium for becoming known. Use a reprint of an article as an excuse to write a professor about his or her work and yours. Say you wanted to present the professor with a copy of your publication because both of you are working in related fields. Do not hesitate to write other professors, even superstars, asking for their advice on your research and publishing projects. This provides you with a chance to introduce yourself and to learn something. They have the opportunity to help you; and most are delighted that someone would flatter them with a plea for help. These letters are a form of advertisement, and some friendships develop by mail. If you follow this correspondence up with prearranged meetings at conventions, close ties can be developed with important scholars—people in a position to help you obtain a good job or research grant. They may also assist your publication role by inviting you to contribute to some project they are chairman of or by telling you of a new journal in need of material.

When publishing material for which you received help, drop a thank-you note into your first footnote acknowledging the help of some scholar(s). Not only will this increase your chances of having the article accepted if you were, for example, aided by an important professor, but it tells the profession the kind of people you associate with. This is strictly public relations work. You benefit by associating yourself with certain key people, and the professors involved have their vanity tickled by unexpectedly seeing their names in print.

You should encourage your major professor to introduce you to as many of the top guns of the profession as possible. This ordinarily happens at conventions or when someone visits your university. If an important professor in your field delivers a lecture at your university, he or she will invariably have a session with the graduate students in the field. Needless to say, you should be there if the lecturer is a member of your profession. And if you have told your professor how badly you want to meet the visitor, he or she can probably make sure that you attend the university function or privately held luncheon or supper for the scholar. The guest may even remember you after leaving campus!

If you or your mentor can negotiate an invitation for you to present a paper at a convention or at a small gathering of scholars from several universities, your name becomes known to a wider audience. Since papers for conventions are planned long in advance, up to a year or more for the big annual affairs, go to your major professor and ask for guidance on how to present a paper. He or she will undoubtedly write the program chairman to describe your topic and to ask if you could prepare it. Or, if you know whom to write, suggest a paper yourself.

Ordinarily, the routine used at most scholarly conventions is the same. Someone of academic stature is made chairman of the small group within which you will be presenting a paper. This may consist of two, three, or even four people talking on related topics. Usually, one person will either read or speak for about twenty to thirty minutes about some dull, obscure project. Then a critic, who has already received a copy of the talk several weeks in advance, rises and finds faults with the paper. Sometimes they are nice and make polite or praiseful comments. Then, either another paper will be given or the audience will be allowed to ask the speaker a few questions about the presentation. Because people are often criticized for whatever they present, the tendency in some fields has been to offer narrower presentations than ever before rather than to introduce some speculative matter which can be subject to severe review. Have your major professor go over your presentation in advance in order to make it as "safe" as possible.

These presentations should be carefully prepared. If you are going to read your paper, make sure that it is well written and short, since everyone will want to hurry the session along and rush back to the bar. You will not need footnotes or much detail. Essentially, you have the job of summarizing your research on a subject; and if people want detail, they will ask for it in the question and answer period. If you handle yourself well in such a session, and important enough scholars are in attendance, you may have done yourself a favor. Do a poor job and a lot of people will remember you as a person to avoid or not to take seriously. You have to be brave if you make a presentation, but you must also ensure that your effort is well done. Besides drawing on professors for advice, you should be very knowledgeable about what you speak on. If you can talk about your thesis or dissertation material, then you are fairly safe, since you will know enough to handle the questions that might be asked.

EXTRACURRICULAR ACTIVITIES

Because your workload is heavy in graduate school, there is little time for extracurricular activities. Other than for personal satisfaction, there are no profession-related reasons for participating in numerous campus and off-campus affairs. Being on the university newspaper staff or in the glee club will not ensure you a good job after graduate school or indicate that you can survive the program. There are exceptions, of course. Obviously, if you are a journalism major, working for the campus newspaper would be a worthy activity, provided that it did not take too much time away from your class work. If you are a music major, coaching the glee club could prove useful professional experience.

The same principle holds for off-campus activities. If you decide to join a political group or a local sports team or help in community charity work, remember that this is time away from your studies. If these efforts are related to your program and do not involve more than a few hours a week, then they may be useful. A social worker major might spend a few hours weekly with underprivileged children, a criminology major might work with delinquents, and an engineering student with the city planning commission. But be aware that many of these activities can cost you valuable time, especially if you are involved in more than one.

If you must involve yourself in non-classroom activities, try to keep them within your profession and, ideally, within the department. Participating in departmental activities will be noted by professors in their letters of recommendation and will indicate to your employers that you work well on a team project. Association with professional organizations and clubs having branches in your department is recommended, since your membership can usually be continued long after you leave school, with professional benefits still accruing. But even with these, remember the time factor. If you find that a local honorary fraternity chapter is involved in a dozen projects, shy away unless you are one of those persons who can complete all your work and still have time for such activities.

There are some general activities that, with some prudence, you can take part in. Such activities will augment your graduate education and will help when you leave school. Membership in pertinent professional and honorary societies and fraternities is nice to have on your record; it is also nice to hold offices in these organizations. You might try to squeeze yourself onto departmental committees formed from the graduate student ranks to advise on program structures, teaching, and student problems. Since students can either be appointed by the faculty or be elected by their peers to these committees, membership indicates to all that you are respected by many of your associates. But again, a word of caution: Do not overextend yourself, since all of these affairs require time.

In some departments, students are encouraged to do career-related work outside of the university rather than within the department. This may include part-time social work for sociology majors, working for the local national park if one is a forestry major, and so on. If you are encouraged to do this and if you want to, try to obtain credit hours for these activities for your permanent transcript. This will indicate to future employers that your education was not just class-oriented.

Some activities do not lend themselves to graduate life because they are too time-consuming or because they are not closely related to your area of specialization. Graduate students, for example, have little time to spend on political activities, especially as leaders. If you are thinking about becoming involved in local civic causes or in backing some political candidate, you will quickly find your time slipping away, with little left for your studies. Although helping a civic cause or supporting a political candidate is very noble and generous, you came to graduate school to subject yourself to a highly disciplined form of education, and this must come first. You have the rest of your life to work with extracurricular activities but only a short while to spend in intensive study.

Furthermore, there is a sad truth to be aware of: If you are involved, for example, in supporting a political candidate, you might alienate a professor who violently dislikes your choice. There is no need to jeopardize yourself in this way. Because you will rarely convert such professors to your views, keep them to yourself, at least until you finish your education.

Many universities sponsor scholarly journals. To be a contributor or to be on the editorial board of one of these looks good on your record and may prove to be a useful, enjoyable experience. Some departments also have journals which are run by their students. In such a case, definitely try to squeeze onto the editorial board and publish through such an outlet.

There is the question of athletics facing many students as well. These can be extremely time-consuming if you are not careful. Fortunately, most intercollegiate athletic associations prohibit graduate students from participating. It is fortunate because this removes temptation from an athletically gifted graduate student. If you want to participate in some activity just for exercise purposes, there is no problem, since you can control the amount of time invested. You might swim, practice your tennis, participate in departmental softball and basketball games, go horseback riding, and play golf. The problem comes if you join a team which meets several times a week for practice. These would include judo and karate groups, and community sponsored ice hockey teams, among others. The one person who can be an exception, even if it means going to graduate school part-time, is the potential Olympic athlete. Here, an unusual situation exists where the love of sport is at least equal to interest in graduate work.

SOCIAL LIFE

For many students at the graduate level, there is less social life than ever before. The style of parties and dating may also undergo changes. Students tend to be in their twenties and early thirties; rarely is there someone under twenty-one around. Many are veterans, while others have worked for several years. A large number are married, either to other graduates or to working spouses. Consequently, graduate social life is under different influences that the undergraduate may not know much about.

Because there is little money available for entertainment, night life is restricted. Movies are popular, but few can afford to visit restaurants often or to go dancing. Usually, students gather in small groups for parties. The people you meet at these are, by and large, people from your department. There is less intermixing of students from various major fields than there is at the under-graduate level. The parties are often small, rarely over a dozen couples.

Sponsored by graduate students as a rule, departmental parties are held several times a year and are large, since most of the graduate students and faculty from one department attend. Whether it is a departmental function or a student's private gathering, ordinarily you will be expected to bring your own bottle unless you are told otherwise. Setups are usually provided, but do not be shy about bringing extras.

Faculty members have parties and dinners to which they invite graduate students. Professors who have farms or large gardens may have picnic-style parties to which everyone brings contributions for the food table. Also, students frequently chip in to buy a keg or two of beer. The end of comps is a popular excuse for this type of party. Because of the weather, these gatherings are ordinarily held in the spring.

Generally, parties follow the adult cocktail type of party, where everyone enjoys a few drinks and some talk. Gone are the days when people would swing from the chandeliers in a fraternity house and dance half-naked in front of a drunk band. Graduate parties are far more sedate affairs. They present opportunities, however, to talk informally with students and professors whom you hardly know. As usual, shop talk dominates, but it can be fun. Rarely do you see any abusive drunkenness.

Major professors invite their students to their homes several times a year. There are some who never do, but most feel that this is part of their responsibility as major professor. When a student passes his or her comps or finishes his dissertation defense, the major professor may invite the graduate over to dinner that night. These and other evenings with your major professor invariably remain quiet ones where both of you can expose facets of your personalities which you cannot reveal at the university. The routine is almost always the same. They all want to show you their libraries, talk about writing in progress, or show slides. Of course, you should show extreme interest even if the evening bores you.

Other professors have parties, usually the cocktail type, and they invite graduate students, whether the students work under them or not. These occasions permit you to develop friendships with professors under whom you have taken courses or with faculty members with whom you never have come in contact. Like graduate parties, they turn into informal rap sessions about department and university-related topics. These are of more than passing interest, however, since you meet people from different departments and find out what is going on in their disciplines and in other parts of your university.

Graduate students date less than undergraduates. There is simply not enough time or money. If you are unmarried, try to find all your dates outside your department. This way, you avoid awkward situations within the department should you break up with someone you dated for a while. You want to stay away from rivalries which may distract you from your work. There is no great status in dating constantly, as there might be at the undergraduate level; and many students hardly date at all. It is more common to spend an evening with someone you meet at a party rather than having a formal date. Everyone is looking for companionship, but time limits the effort that can go into this search.

Single student teachers often find dates, and sometimes they find their spouses, in the classes they teach. It is a good idea not to date anyone who is taking a course under you. Avoid both conflicts of interest and being the subject of a few jokes and nasty insinuations. Wait until the course is over. If you keep your personal life semiprivate, you save yourself problems.

A large number of inexpensive activities take place on all campuses, and at large universities there is at least one event each day. If you are dating or if you just want to go out, there is no lack of things to do. For examples, recent movies are shown, often either for free admission or for about fifty cents; and plays, musical concerts, ballets, art shows, fairs, athletic events, speeches by politicians, and lectures by outstanding scholars occur all the time. Many campuses have their own tea and coffee shops, complete with live entertainment, Your university newspaper lists all of these events. Often, you can buy season tickets to groups of activities for a few dollars. Purchasing a season pass may be the only way to see cultural events, since season ticket holders frequently will fill all the seats in an auditorium, leaving no tickets for sale at the box office.

The loneliness of a graduate student single is often unique and intense. Although dates as such provide some relief, seeing the same faces from your department does not. If you can, try to establish purely social friendships outside the department, perhaps even away from the university, and do this as soon as possible. It acts as a welcome change. If you are married, develop friendships with, for example, a wife's colleagues.

Since most graduate students like to avoid the sterility of dorm life, they live in apartments—often with a roommate—or they form a group and rent a house. This is an excellent way to meet people outside of your department, and you should exploit this source for friends. Such a living arrangement provides a respite from graduate studies. But if you live with several people, make sure that you have a room where you can go to study whenever the urge hits you, because students maintain weird hours and study patterns and often these will clash with your way of doing things.

If you find that graduate school affects your psychological makeup, or that the pressures involved make life uncomfortable, or if you have problems with a companion or spouse, most campuses have a psychologist in residence at the university's medical center. Graduate school can affect people quite seriously; consequently, do not hesitate to seek medical or psychological attention. If your friends cannot help, and if the problem is not serious enough to warrant medical attention, you may find that leaving town during a quarter or semester break may be the solution to your concern. Some students just become book-saturated and need to stop working for a while and get away from reading. This can be an excuse for leaving books behind and taking off, possibly with some friends, for a beach or a different city or for home. A change of scenery occasionally is important, because graduate students tend to go to school year round, while undergraduates leave campus at every opportunity. Socially, deserting your campus for a few days will be refreshing. Temporarily, at least, you can put shoptalk in the back closet.

MEDICAL AND INSURANCE PROBLEMS

When you come to graduate school, you face the problems of finding medical aid and of buying medical insurance, even if you are in perfect health. If you are married and have children, the issue becomes more imperative. Although the following discussion is not a detailed study of the insurance industry, you should be aware of a few facts.

If you were previously covered by a family medical policy paid for by your parents, read the policy. Many family insurance plans provide no coverage for children when they reach the age of twenty-one or twenty-two. If your family's policy is one of these, you will have to buy new medical insurance. If you worked or spent time in the armed services, and in both cases were protected by company or military plans, these may no longer be in force for you, or their period of coverage could have a deadline. Therefore, check these policies.

Three options lie open to you if you must purchase new medical insurance. First, you can enroll in a university medical insurance plan. These cost little and usually have a small lump sum that will be paid upon your death if it occurs while you are a student. Some of these plans may be extended to cover your immediate family as well. Second, you can buy Blue Cross and Blue Shield insurance for you and your family. Since you will be a student, this particular plan will be offered to you at a reduced rate. The third option is to purchase medical coverage from regular commercial insurance companies, some of which give discounts to students. Whatever arrangement appeals to you, make some provision for insurance, since academic life is no guarantee of good health.

Obtaining a doctor's service poses many problems. Most doctors today are overloaded with patients and add new ones to their lists reluctantly, especially in a university town where there are never enough physicians. To find a physician check the yellow pages of the telephone book, ask friends for names, and contact the student union. Make your appointment early, because you will often have to wait for several months. This advice also applies to eye doctors and, especially, to dentists. Before selecting your doctors, check with a few students and professors to find out who they recommend. You will quickly learn to stay away from some, either because they overcharge or because people lack confidence in them. In order to become a patient quickly, make an appointment for an ordinary physical. This way, when you have an emergency situation or when you become ill, you will be on a doctor's list of clients. In the choice of a general practitioner, find out who your professors recommend rather than listening to the students, since the former have lived in town longer and know the local doctors.

Your university will invariably have either a fancy infirmary or a medical college. As a student, you will be entitled to draw upon the services of these medical facilities, either for free or at low cost. Often, this also applies to a student's immediate family. At least, you can usually fill your prescriptions here at rates far lower than at any of the local drugstores. And although at small campuses, the local college doctor is often maligned, at a university, few students would question the reliability of the infirmary's physicians. By using them for some of your aches and pains and, of course, for emergency reasons, you can reduce your medical expenses. The paper work involved also melts away if you have your insurance with the university's group policy.

YOU AND THE LAW

As a student you may have recourse to the law, due to some grievance on your part or because you violated a statute. Many universities still have regulations stipulating that a student convicted of a felony or, in some cases, of a misdemeanor, must be expelled from school. Others limit this to felonies.

If you feel that your civil liberties have been violated, either by the university or by someone in town and you cannot afford a lawyer to redress grievances, contact the local branch of the American Civil Liberties Union. Often this organization has a campus representative, either at the law school (if your university has one) or among the faculty. If the representative is a teacher, his or her name will often be listed in the university phone book as the A.C.L.U. representative. They are also listed in the local directory. Some schools also offer limited free legal advice; you might keep this in mind. If you can afford to hire a lawyer, remember, especially if you are from out-of-state, that an attorney must be licensed to practice in the state where legal action takes place. Therefore, your family lawyer back home may only give you advice and may have no authorization to practice in the state you live in.

Many students will tell you soon after your arrival that businesses and local police dislike students and abuse them at every opportunity. Furthermore, they may indicate which local businesses cheat. The local bank may possibly treat you with mistrust, and students will argue that the police fine and arrest students in violation of their rights. This may or may not be true in your university town, although chances are that some hostility is directed toward students by various citizens of the town. You may have found this out as an undergraduate. But judge for yourself by what happens to you before castigating the entire community. If, however, someone cheats or seriously wrongs you, redress exists.

One of the easiest ways students are cheated and bothered is by the door-to-door salesmen who seem to thrive in university towns. If you live in an apartment, you see dozens of these people before you finish graduate work, and you will probably purchase items from them. If one cheats you, contact the local consumer service bureau or better business office and register a complaint. Often, if the bureau finds a serious abuse, it will move to curb the menace. Since these consumer protection agencies come under various titles, you may have some difficulty locating them. Call the local chamber of commerce for their names. If this fails, telephone the home economics department on campus. Hopefully, someone there will know whom you must contact. If you live in a state capital, the state department of agriculture or commerce probably has a division for consumer protection.

As another recourse, contact your campus newspaper. Many university newspapers publicize the activities of dishonest merchants and expose illegal practices in order to warn students. And if you feel that your civil liberties have really been slighted, call the American Civil Liberties Union. They will give you advice on your legal options.

Automobile tags and voter registration are two other ways students generally come into contact with the law. In most states, students do not have to purchase new automobile tags or driver's licenses or adhere to local insurance requirements as long as they claim out-of-state citizenship. Once you declare yourself a local resident (usually after one year's residence in the state) or you become eligible to vote, then you must abide by local regulations regarding tags, licenses, and insurance. You might check into your automobile insurance, however, if you move into a state that has no-fault car insurance to make sure your current policy applies in that state. If you work, or if your spouse does, in the state in which you go to school, you will probably have ninety days in which to change your car tags, driver's licenses, and insurance policy. For local regulations, call the nearby state police office. Also, if you work in the state, you may have to pay state income tax, so check that as well. For voter registration information, call the town, city, or county registrar of voters or the court clerk.

TIPS ON FOOD PURCHASES

Many people come to graduate school with little or no experience in food shopping, having spent four years eating in college cafeterias or as dinner guests of one of the armed services. Few students have had to live for a while on their own, purchasing all their food. Like any other expensive yet necessary activity, grocery purchasing is a time-consuming activity which digs deeply into your limited funds; yet home economists generally agree that there are some fundamental rules one can follow in order to reduce food costs.

In order to stretch your food dollar, shop after you have eaten. If you arrive at the grocery store starving to death, everything will look good; consequently, you will buy more than you need. Plan a week's menus before you go marketing in order to avoid needless purchases. In planning meals, check newspaper ads for weekly specials, since they can save you a few dollars each week. After planning your menus and reading the ads, draw up a shopping list. Check the supplies you have on hand in order to reduce excess purchases. If you can get into the habit of immediately writing down items as you use them up, you will save time when preparing your list. Once you make up your order, do not forget to take it with you to the store! Then plan to give yourself sufficient time to shop. If you rush, you will forget to buy key items, and snap decisions will cost you extra money.

A large percentage of food money spent by Americans goes for meat. In order to reduce this expense, compare the actual amount of lean to the amount of waste (bone, fat, and gristle) in each pound. Judge the value of a piece of meat by the cost per serving rather than by the cost per pound. A less expensive cut that has lots of bone and fat may cost more than a higher priced boneless cut. A pound of ground meat will yield more servings than a pound of spare ribs. In judging servings, try the following guide:

Meat without bone	¼ pound per serving
Meat with little bone	½ pound per serving
Meat with a lot of bone	¾ to 1 pound per serving

When shopping for meat, always consider these lower cost meats: ground and stewing meats; pork roasts; lamb, veal and ham shanks; chicken; variety meats, such as liver, heart, kidney, tongue, tripe, brains, and sweetbreads; and canned meats. Always buy well-trimmed meat, otherwise you will be paying the same amount for fat as you do for lean. Study the amount of meat per serving, because most Americans eat more than they need. Nutrition experts suggest that a serving should be about three ounces of lean cooked meat. Also consider meat alternatives, such as eggs, dry beans, and peanut butter, in planning your meals.

Other handy points to be aware of would include stretching meat with beans, peas, macaroni, rice, potatoes, and vegetables. Purchase ground beef in large packages, because this is cheaper than in small quantities. Packages weighing more than five pounds ordinarily cost three to five cents less per pound than smaller sizes. Less tender cuts of steak, such as chuck, bottom round, or shoulder steak, can be purchased occasionally without breaking your budget. Variety meats such as liver and kidney are less expensive than regular cuts of meat and have high nutritive value. Serving liver is both inexpensive and good for your health. If you buy liver, you will find that pork and chicken livers are the cheapest. If your refrigerator is not too small, buy whole chickens and cut them up at home to save on the cost per pound. And, talking about chicken, you should plan on three-quarters to one pound as a serving. Turkey is another bargain all year; the larger the bird you buy, the more meat it will have in proportion to bone. Pork shoulder steak, similar to pork chops in appearance and flavor, often costs less than chops.

As meat substitutes, eggs and dairy products are excellent. They save you money and provide variety in your meals. There are three grades of eggs that you should be aware of: Grades AA and A, which are best for frying and poaching because of their size, and Grade B, which is just as nutritious as the other grades but is more suitable for scrambling and putting in baking products. The biggest difference lies in the expense: AA eggs are the most expensive, while B eggs cost the least. Fresh and cultured milk costs more than the dried and canned variety; and the cheapest product is made from nonfat dry milk.

In purchasing fruits and vegetables, buy those which are in season for the greatest savings. Canned or frozen vegetables cost more than the fresh varieties in season. In selecting the quality and form (fresh, canned, whole) of fruits and vegetables, consider how you will use them. For example, if you use peppers in a salad, buy those which have been reduced for quick sale. They may be smaller and withered looking, but the taste and nutritive value remains the same.

Remember that prices are not necessarily guides to good choices. It is often more important that you determine the price per serving than the cost per pound or bunch. Quantity food purchases result in savings if ample storage space is available. If you do not have adequate facilities, such as a freezer, having too much food on hand can be wasteful, since it will spoil. Pre-prepared foods always cost more than if you cook them yourself. You can also save money by purchasing a large piece of meat and cutting it up yourself for stews, goulashes, and meat pies. The same holds true for poultry. Combine your beans and franks. Slice and grate your own cheese. The packaging and preslicing of cold cuts almost doubles their price. Since snack foods are very expensive, you would do better to eat celery sticks or a raw carrot. Store brands frequently sell at lower prices than some name products and may be just as satisfactory in terms of quality. Try to become familiar with these store brands, because on occasion special sales of these items save you money. Buy day-old bread; it is just as good as the bread you have kept in your bread box for a couple of days.

At home, you can also stretch your food dollar. Refrigerate leftover vegetables in a "soup pot," and at the end of the week, you will have a first course to some meal. Save on utilities by planning meals that can be cooked entirely in the oven or under the broiler. Consider cooking for two or more meals when you make a dish requiring much preparation. If you buy meat with a bone, have the butcher remove it or do that yourself; always save it for the soup pot. Melt down fat trimmings for drippings. Adjust your menus when there are leftovers. Do not pour your money down the drain. With a little creativity, yesterday's leftovers can be an attractive meal today. Avoid desserts as often as possible; they only increase your food budget and your waistline.

Because students have become heavy users of organic foods, they should be aware that mislabeled organic foods do exist and that these are more expensive than other organic foods. If you buy organic foods, purchase them at a place which your friends or professors know from experience is reliable. Check organic food labels in order to determine how the foods were raised and processed and for comments on pesticide and additive uses. Observe with care what so-called breakfast food cereals contain. Many are not organically grown and will have the same contents as nonorganic products. The same holds true for juices. Be careful on your choice of vitamins as well. In fact, you might have a doctor recommend a brand, since many have incorrect proportions and can threaten your health.

Treat organic purchases as you would regular grocery chores. Compare prices at several stores. Avoid organic toothpastes, hair shampoos, cosmetics, and raw sugar, because there are many nonorganic items being sold under this popular rubric at exorbitant prices. If you are worried about some product, write the manufacturer for details about the processing of the item. If you receive no answer or if you get some hot air, mistrust the product. For the pricing of organic foods, watch the food pages of your Sunday newspaper. Because of its current popularity, the subject is often discussed. You can then see if you are being cheated by a local merchant. If you are, stop patronizing him.

6

Obtaining Employment

FINDING A JOB

Consider the type of work you want before you go to graduate school in order to determine the kind of further training you will need, if any. But if you are already in graduate school and will soon be looking for employment, you again face the question of employment. This issue revolves around two points: First, do you want to work in the field in which you did your advanced study or second, do you want to work in some area that has no direct relationship to your schooling? The second is often the most unpopular alternative, but is is becoming more realistic as some fields become swamped with M.A.s and Ph.D.s, thus forcing students to seek employment elsewhere. Those who wish to work in the area of their training may find their fields glutted if they view their career goals only in terms of teaching. Even within one branch of knowledge, a person needs to consider various forms of employment.

If you were perceptive enough to choose a minor field outside of your department, thus giving you a more diversified background, your job opportunities may well be enhanced. Flexibility is sought after by governmental, industrial, and educational employers. Consequently, think of your background and options in the broadest possible terms. This is especially recommended for someone with an M.B.A., since the alternatives in the business world are so diverse. If you want to teach, sell yourself with as many different fields as you can, because an employer would rather hire one person to teach several diverse courses than employ two or more specialists.

For those aspiring to teach, some general comments can be made. People having just the M.A. should plan to teach at the elementary, high school, or, possibly, junior college levels. In fact, elementary and high schools will rarely hire the Ph.D. Prep schools are also leery. With Ph.D. in hand, one can teach in a junior college, a college, or a university, assuming that job openings exist. Usually, the more education you have, the more money one assumes you will be paid. Today, however, the number of Ph.D.s seeking employment is so large that starting pay scales may actually go down and certainly will not increase appreciably. But this varies in each subject area and at every level of education.

You might consider employment as a researcher or as an administrator in your field. Natural science people might try research institutes and government agencies for jobs, while a social scientist might work for an archive, newspaper, or a public opinion survey group. There are managerial positions to consider applying for, especially since many graduate students discount bureaucratic jobs. But remember that government positions pay well.

Some students have found that they were overeducated for some jobs. Some employers feel that they cannot retrain an old dog or that M.A. and Ph.D. graduates will soon leave them for teaching positions. Also, a Ph.D. usually wants more money than a M.A., and someone's budget may not be loose enough to accomodate even this small an increase in salary costs.

There are several ways to find out about job openings. Consult your professors, since they hear about jobs in their fields. A word of caution is needed here, however. Many professors want their students only to go into college and university teaching, which becomes a way an academician's ideas are advanced. Be aware of this motive. If someone in your department has knowledge of and contacts with employers seeking people in related areas, go to him or her for advice and aid in obtaining one of these jobs. Often, the difference between a person finding employment and the other being turned down revolves around knowing someone who is influential with an employer.

As a rule, departments will make some efforts to find employment for their graduate students. This push for jobs takes many forms. Professors who know people hiring student for teaching, for research or for other related work write letters and make phone calls praising their student's virtues. Mailing lists of recent graduates, with a summary of their backgrounds, to universities, government agencies, and industries accounts for another popular technique, although it is less effective. Frequently, departments make sure that students register their names and résumés with profession-wide organizations, which often publish job registers citing open positions and the names of those desiring employment. Departments also encourage their students to attend professional conventions in search of jobs.

Another source of jobs is the university's employment office. Although many of these claim to be career counseling services whose purpose is to show students the kind of careers they can pursue given their educational background, many others simply view themselves as employment agencies. Either way, these university offices can be of great use to you. They make arrangements for recruiters from industry and government to come on campus to talk with prospective employees, between October and May of each year. They publish schedules of recruiters' visits in brochures and in the campus newspaper; they keep on file information about various careers which students can examine; and they encourage students to leave with them a résumé and letters of recommendation which can be photocopied and mailed to interested employers. They will do much of the paper work involved in having students interviewed by potential employers recruiting on campus. Such offices also have a generous supply of application forms for government jobs and for various tests. Other counselors pepper certain industries with announcements regarding their recent graduates. Therefore, in looking for jobs, consult your career counselor.

In some universities, a school or a group of departments will pool their employment efforts together and have their own career counseling office apart from the university's. This is a common practice with business, medical, and law schools. Such a system provides unusual recruiting procedures which may not lend themselves to the university as a whole. Using business schools as an example, one can see the prognosis for employment. Business schools will approach major corporations seeking monetary donations for the university and, more importantly, for the school. In return, such a donating firm will be allowed to recruit among the graduates before the rest of the nation's companies are asked to do so. This practice, common at the more prestigious universities, virtually ensures that business graduates will find employment, since hundreds of companies contribute money for the privilege of recruiting new employees.

The extent of this procedure, hardly known by educators, is not even admitted to by many companies. Stanford University publicly states that companies annually give $500,000 to their business school. Bethlehem Steel Corporation's vice president, Laurence Fenninger, Jr., stated, in the June 14, 1972 issue of the *New York Times*, that between 1953 and 1972 his company contributed $8.5 million to at least 150 schools. During the past decade, Kodak gave away more than $30 million. Consequently, at least in the business world, jobs exist in great numbers; and students should consider these opportunities.

State employment agencies and the Veterans Administration publish monthly bulletins concerning jobs; these bulletins are available at the campus career counseling office. Some universities, colleges, and other educational institutions also publish lists of openings, as, for example, do the junior colleges in Virginia. Most professions have a job register which they publish several times a year and which can be found in all appropriate departments or in the counselor's office. For ideas on available jobs, you might consult the U.S. Department of Labor's publication, *Occupational Outlook Handbook*, which is published in even years. This supplies information on what fields will have expansion in the next few years and which will shrink. This book predicted that Ph.D.s would be overabundant throughout the 1980s. The demand for local, state, and federal government personnel will rapidly increase, as will the demand for skilled craftsmen and for clerical and vocational people.

Other sources of information on jobs include your friends and family, because many people looking for new employees do not publicize that fact. Since openings spread by word of mouth, you must check with people you know for ideas. If you have developed any professional relationships while in school with people you feel could be asked for jobs, by all means write or call them to see what they can do. Perhaps an uncle knows someone who could hire you. These sources are often some of the best available to you, especially if your field is glutted and you need to look at new horizons.

Since you must actively seek employment by your own means, rather than with hopes pinned on someone else's efforts, do not hesitate to blitz a region or an industry with letters asking about openings. When you do this, describe your background and possibly enclose a brief résumé. You will have to write people in more than just three or four states; and you must be prepared, if need be, to mail several hundred letters in a short period of time. Out of such a pile, a few job possibilities may develop. Start your campaign early, at least four or five months before you intend to finish your degree, because landing a good job takes time and effort.

CONVENTIONS

Because conventions are an important source for jobs, especially in the academic world and in certain skilled fields such as home economics and engineering, they deserve special attention. As a rule, students do not attend conventions to see exhibits or to hear papers read. These gatherings are slave markets where graduates come to find jobs.

All conventions have more or less the same format. From several weeks to a couple of months before a meeting, people begin to make hotel reservations and register for a convention. Usually, a committee reserves hotel space and provides forms which students can mail to them, describing their backgrounds and the types of jobs they desire. Once at the convention, students register, leaving extra résumés for the recruitment program. Many employers will make arrangements with the registration desk to have appointments set up with prospective employees. Often, a student simply signs up for a vacant interview time period and then goes to the interviewer's hotel room for a talk. Some students make appointments in advance by mail with interested recruiters.

Wealthy departments have cocktail parties to which professors from other schools come, along with recruiters and people looking for jobs. This gives the host department a chance to talk to those searching for positions and allows faculty members to visit with friends from other schools. Should an interesting person catch the eye of the host department's interviewer, further meetings are arranged with one or more faculty members from the same department. Your major professor may take you to several of these parties in order to introduce you to friends who might be interested in hiring you. Companies also have cocktail parties for recruitment purposes. Whether for industry or education, the parties provide excellent opportunities for an extrovert student to mingle, to meet potential employers, and, possibly, to impress one of them enough to make a job offer.

Competition for positions, always fierce at these conventions, appears to be on the increase. At some gatherings in the recent past, students have raided the job registration desk to steal and destroy résumé sheets in order to reduce competition. These desks may now be guarded, since many recruiters study résumés first before asking to speak to job seekers. Because so many people look for work at a convention, finding an opportunity to talk alone with a prospective employer can often be nearly impossible. Try to arrange a meeting by mail before you come to the convention. If you have not done this preliminary footwork, attempt to make an appointment by telephone once you arrive at the hotel. The third way to see someone is to take a chance that, during the interviewing process, they may have a slack in work and that you will get a few minutes to talk. Some major professors do ensure that their people have that opportunity.

Some students waste time at conventions when looking for employment. Obviously, the average graduate student should not try to seek a job with one of the top schools in the country without having done some preliminary negotiating. Yet you will see many stream off to the departmental parties given by Harvard, Princeton, Yale, and others, hoping that something will develop. Be more realistic. Find out at the job registration desk who needs people with your qualifications and then go to those you feel might have an interest in you. At the general meetings of the convention, and later in bars and restaurants, try to meet with professors and students who are working for other departments. These are good sources of information about unannounced jobs.

Even if you are not looking for positions, you should at least talk to people working in your area of specialization. Such contacts are invaluable if you plan an academic career, since they may hire you in the future, and since they may be asked to comment on your manuscripts for publishers and, later, to review them for journals. They will have a hand in deciding if you should receive grants, awards, and positions as editorial advisors to various projects. Professors and people in industry also use conventions to find out what everyone else in the profession is doing. You should do the same. In one day at a convention, you can learn more about what goes on in your profession than in months of letter writing.

An interesting pecking order exists at conventions, and it is quickly discernable, even by a novice. Unknown people in your profession seek after important professors. The superstars try to mingle among themselves, while the lesser knowns attempt to crash into this tight circle, hoping that the big men will remember in the future. Some people simply like to be seen associating with a famous member of their profession. They will keep one eye on you during conversation and the other roaming around to see if someone more important has come into the room. Once that happens, you will be left cold, standing there alone with your hands in your pockets, as your conversationalist rushes forward to meet the superstar. Individuals do this when they are in search of jobs or advice, or in order to be seen with the beautiful people, or to work business deals. Although it may sometimes create ludicrous situations, you should be aware of this behavior pattern. Once you become famous, people will be constantly bugging you at conventions.

Besides looking for jobs and trying to impress people with your personality and erudition, other convention interests can occupy your time. In addition to bar hopping with colleagues, friends, and professors, you can attend some of the sessions to hear papers read on topics of interest to you. Many publishers have booths set up where you can obtain free copies of their publications. Some companies are less generous and only display their wares. Corporations exhibit new products and often give free samples—or at least literature on them—away. If you are in some city that has a major library, archive, or research institute, take advantage of your geographic situation to visit them. If you have some specific research in mind that can be done there because they have a unique collection, go and examine the materials. You might find that the items can be microfilmed and sent to you after the convention closes.

Traveling to a convention can be expensive if you are not careful. Most students cannot afford to take an airplane to the convention city and then pay an exorbitant price for a room just to find a job.

If the convention is not too far away from your campus, you might organize a car pool of three or four students to drive there, sharing expenses for gas, oil, and tolls. If there are enough people from your department going, suggest chartering a bus. In order to do this, however, at least twenty-five people will have to go. This, too, is inexpensive and can be fun. Some well-funded departments help pay travel expenses for their students, but ordinarily this happens only after all faculty expressing an interest in attending the convention have received travel funds. It should be noted, however, that most departments do not finance graduate students' travel expenses.

Staying in a convention city is expensive, no matter how you arrange your accommodations. Ordinarily housed in one hotel, conventions may occupy two or three. If more than one person from your department goes, try to share a room with a fellow student. Professors rarely will "lower" themselves to room with a student, even though it would almost make their hotel bill reasonable. If you have a friend or relative living in town, try to stay with him or her and really save money. Think twice before eating all your meals in the hotel restaurant, since you may do better in neighboring places. Check the menu; many hotel restaurants charge more than other local establishments. Although this is not a general rule, it is common in many convention hotels. You may find, on the other hand, that because of a convention being held in a particular hotel, you can rent a room with one or more meals for a reasonable combination price. Hotels can do this where they are guaranteed a certain minimum amount of business. But whatever accommodations you decide upon, do so in advance. If you choose to stay at a less expensive hotel than the one where the convention meets, confirm reservations in advance, since other people will have the same idea.

OVEREDUCATION AND EMPLOYMENT

All your life you have been told to go to college in order to obtain good employment. You have probably read in newspapers how various government surveys shows that better educated people make more money than their less enlightened colleagues. The cold hard fact remains, however, that there is such a problem as being overeducated and that it can have a decisive, negative effect on your employment prospects. Although some mention of this problem has already been made in passing, you need to be more aware of it, since most students do not consider the issue until they begin seeking employment. When the ugly truth hits them that a Ph.D. may actually cramp their chances for employment, students become cynical, shocked, and bewildered as they see their hard work net dismal returns.

During the late 1960s and the 1970s, graduate schools in the United States produced more Ph.D.s in virtually every field than the number of jobs available for doctoral graduates. This has been a rude shock to graduate schools, to students, and to their potential employers. Practically every major area of study groans under the weight of graduate programs that overproduce students. It takes time for graduate schools to cut back their programs, and some are doing so; but in the meanwhile, universities continue to entice students to continue on for higher degrees. Professors and nonacademicians, not fully aware of the doctoral glut, also continue to advise students to continue on with their education. You should be cognizant of this condition. There is probably little malicious intent involved, and, more likely than not, the crisis is a reflection of ignorance and the current job market for Ph.D.s seeking traditional employment.

Although the United States could reach the point where a government program for employing these highly educated people may have to be implemented, as was partially done during the depression of the 1930s, students should not count on this. Those who would like to continue teaching in higher education must realize that the World War II baby boom is over and that the Korean War baby crop is a pale shadow of the former. Demographic experts say that the college population is stabilizing and that it will probably not experience any appreciable growth until the late 1980s. That is a long time for anyone to wait around for a good teaching job. As the only solution to this employment crisis, one must reconsider what to study in graduate school. Also ask yourself what you will do with yourself after you have finished with university studies.

One might begin, as some now do, to view a year or more of graduate study as a cultural finishing school that smooths out the rough edges left by undergraduate work. If you treat graduate education as a humanistic experience or as an intellectual tune-up, then you approach the employment problem far differently than the person who is essentially learning a teaching trade. The former will be able to conceptualize more broadly the kind of employment he or she would accept, even to the point of applying for jobs requiring no use of learned skills and at salaries that five or ten years ago would have been repudiated by a Ph.D. Many students, especially at the M.A. level, consider one or two years of graduate school merely as a slight extension of college days. This is a healthy view for one to take today. Thus, someone with a Ph.D. in education might consider working for a major corporation while another with an M.A. in child counseling might seek employment as a personnel director in a state prison system.

The individual who emerges from graduate school with the idea that he or she has learned a trade, such as teaching in one specialized area at the college and university level, may find no job. To this person, one could say today he or she is overeducated for the current needs of society. Most students would like to work in the area in which they received their education, but that is becoming increasingly difficult to do in many fields today.

If you can decide which personal characteristics you have developed in school, what specific skills you have learned, and how your ideas about yourself and society have matured, you will find that your options become virtually limitless. Decide if you want a competitive career, and make up your mind about where you want to live, whether in a rural or urban area, and whether you wish to live by the pen or as a bureaucrat. With some ideas worked out in your mind, you may find that your graduate education was a worthy experience, possible because at its conclusion it made you think about your future with some degree of confidence and wisdom.

If you have learned a few things that can be pointed out to yourself, a start has been made in the reassessment. There are some obvious points of departure. Even if you spent only one year in graduate school, it is hoped you have been made to think about many things. You have done heavy reading, requiring responses by you. You wrote papers that had some cohesion. In all probability, others' ideas have forced you to contemplate and react. As a corollary, you have been exposed to the way one should try to view information and ideas, with the sense of objectivity necessary in any honest intellectual exercise.

Most students have to do a great deal of writing in graduate school. One could spend a year in advanced study and write no more than you would in a year of undergraduate work, but this is rare. If you have to write anything, you need to think and express yourself with a modicum of clarity and with respect for English grammar. For some, using a dictionary has been a new experience, while for others, finally learning what paragraphs and dangling modifiers are was a major accomplishment. This practical skill, no matter how rudimentarily developed, continues to be important in our paper-conscious society. We generate more red tape than ever before. Hardly anyone working today can avoid filling out forms and writing reports. In many jobs, publishing is a part of the work requirement, forcing many people to compose more and better than ever before. Success in many positions depends on clear writing. Therefore, you might think in terms of a career that uses your writing skills, even if the job you have in mind has no relation to the field in which you did your graduate work.

Only two suggestions have been offered about the sort of assets one can look for in his or her background. Both transcend narrow fields such as history, biology, English, physics, economics, and psychology. Search for fundamental, marketable qualities in yourself. Do not let your degrees imprison your imagination. And remember that there is always a job for you. The only problem you have is to find it.

Obtaining
Employment

Bibliography

PROGRAM DESCRIPTIONS

NESS, FREDERIC W. *A Guide to Graduate Study: Programs Leading to the Ph.D. Degree.* Washington, D.C.: Association of American Colleges, 1960.

QUICK, ROBERT (ed.) *A Guide to Graduate Study: Programs Leading to the Ph.D. Degree.* Washington, D.C.: American Council on Education, 1969. This book lists the programs of 250 universities as they are listed in their catalogues; cost: $15.00.

Study Abroad. New York: UNESCO. Published periodically; cost: about $6.00.

WALTERS, EVERETT. *Graduate Education Today.* Washington, D.C.: American Council on Education, 1965.

STUDENT TEACHING

McKEACHIE, W.J. *Teaching Tips: A Guide-Book for the Beginning College Teacher.* Ann Arbor: George WAHR Publishing Co., 1965.

NOWLIS, VINCENT. *The Graduate Student As Teacher.* Washington, D.C.: American Council on Education, 1968.

GUIDES TO FIELDS OF GRADUATE WORK

American Psychological Association. *Graduate Study in Psychology.* This is an annual publication costing about 50¢. For copies, write the American Psychological Association, 1200 17th St., N.W., Washington, D.C. 20036.

"American Studies Program," usually published in the summer supplement of the *American Quarterly* each year. For copies, costing under $2.00, write the American Studies Association, Box 30, Bennett Hall, University of Pennsylvania, Philadelphia, Pennsylvania 19104.

Colleges and Universities in the United States Offering Instruction in Forestry. This annual publication is given away free by the Society of American Foresters, Suite 300, 1010 16th St., N.W., Washington, D.C. 20036

Engineering College Research and Graduate Study. This annual directory may be purchased by students for under $5.00 from the American Society for Engineering Education, 2100 Pennsylvania Avenue, Washington, D.C. 20037.

Graduate Programs in Physics and Astronomy. A Handbook For Advisors of Prospective Doctoral and Masters Students. A recent edition sold for about $5.00 and may be purchased from the American Institute of Physics, 335 E. 45th St., New York, New York 10017.

Graduate Study in Economics. Revised periodically, this may be obtained by writing Richard D. Irwin, Inc., 1818 Ridge Rd., Homewood, Illinois 60430.

Guide to Departments of Anthropology for the Year . . . . Revised annually, the cost is about $2.00 and the publication covers departments in the U.S.A., Mexico, and Canada. For copies, write the American Anthropological Association, 1703 New Hampshire Ave., Washington, D.C. 20009.

Guide to Graduate Study in Botany. Published in 1968 by the Botanical Society of America, this guide sells for $3.00. To obtain copies, write Richard C. Starr, Department of Botany, Indiana University, Bloomington, Indiana 47401.

HENDERSON, BONNIE C. (ed.) *Directory of Geoscience Departments*. Published in even years, this directory sells for about $9.00 and may be purchased from the American Geological Institute, 2201 M. St., N.W., Washington, D.C. 20037. The book discusses programs in geology, geophysics, and oceanography.

Planning for Graduate Work in Chemistry. Costing less than $1.00, this guide is revised periodically and may be obtained from the American Chemical Society, Committee on Professional Training, 343 State St., Rochester, New York, 14650.

Research Specialties of Doctoral Programs in Physics and Astronomy. New York: American Institute of Physics, 1968; free.

Road to Graduate School in Engineering. Published in 1967, this book can be obtained from the American Society for Engineering Education, 2100 Pennsylvania Avenue, Washington, D.C. 20037.

SCHWENDEMAN, J.R. *et al.* (eds.) *Directory of College Geography of the United States: Academic Year . . . .* Costing about $1.00, this directory may be purchased from the Association of American Geographers, c/o Geographical Studies and Research Center, Eastern Kentucky University, Richmond, Kentucky 40475.

University Resources for Linguistics in the United States and Canada. This detailed study costs about $2.00 and may be purchased from the Center for Applied Linguistics, 1717 Massachusetts Ave., N.W., Washington, D.C. 20036.

FINANCIAL AID

A Manual for Obtaining Government Grants and *A Manual for Obtaining Foundation Grants.* Free copies may be obtained from Robert J. Corcoran Co., 40 Court St., Boston, Massachusetts 02108.

ANGEL, JUVENAL L. *How and Where to Get Scholarships and Loans.* New York: Regents Publishing Co., 1968. This is available at most college book stores for about $3.50.

BROWNSTEIN, SAMUEL C. AND MITCHEL WEINER. *You Can Win a Scholarship.* Woodbury, N.Y.: Barron's Educational Series, 1972. This is available at most college book stores for about $5.95.

Council for European Studies. *Fellowship Guide for Western Europe.* Pittsburgh, Pennsylvania, periodically published. For free copies, write to the Council for European Studies, 213 Social Science Bldg., University of Pittsburgh, Pittsburgh, Pennsylvania 15213.

Financial Assistance for Library Education. Write to the American Library Association, 50 East Huron St., Chicago, Illinois 60611.

Journalism Scholarship Guide. Princeton, N.J.: Newspaper Fund, Inc., 1969. Write Newspaper Fund, Box 400, Princeton, New Jersey 08540 for this free, detailed booklet.

National Institutes of Health. *Research Fellowships. Announcements of Predoctoral, Postdoctoral, or Special Research Fellowship Programs.* Bethesda, Md.: The Institutes. This free publication is available from Career Development Review Branch, Division of Research Grants, NIH, Bethesda, Maryland 20014, and is broken up by fields.

National Opinion Research Center. *Stipends and Spouses; The Finances of American Arts and Science Graduate Students.* Chicago: University of Chicago Press, 1962.

National Science Foundation. *Graduate Fellowships.* Washington, D.C.: NSF; annual and free.

———. *Graduate Traineeships.* Washington, D.C.: NSF; annual and free.

Office of Education. *Awards for Modern Foreign Language and Area Study.* Washington, D.C.: U.S. Government Printing Office; annual; under $1.00.

———. *National Defense Graduate Fellowships: Graduate Programs.* Washington, D.C.: U.S. Government Printing Office; annual and free. Write the Division of Graduate Programs, Bureau of Higher Education, Washington, D.C. 20202.

Post-Baccalaureate Grants and Awards in Music. Periodically revised and for sale at about $1.00, this guide may be obtained from Music Educators National Conference, 1201 16th St., N.W., Washington, D.C. 20036.

SCANNELL, W.J. (ed.) *Directory of Assistantships and Fellowships for Graduate Study in English and the Teaching of English.* This annual publication may be purchased for about $3.00 from the National Council of Teachers of English, 508 South Sixth St., Chicago, Illinois 61820.

WALKER, GORDON L. *Assistantships and Fellowships in Mathematics.* This annual publication may be obtained from the American Mathematics Society, 321 S. Main St., Providence, Rhode Island 02904.

Woodrow Wilson National Fellowship Foundation. For information, write the Foundation, Box 642, Princeton, New Jersey 08540.

Index

149

Index